Y0-CQQ-781

# The Rebel King

*By the same author*
Documents of Liberty
Dark Age Britain
The Caesars
Slavery and Race
The Rebel King: The story of Christ as Seen Against the Historical Conflict Between the Roman Empire and Judaism

*As Beram Saklatvala*
The Christian Island
Arthur: Roman Britain's Last Champion
The Origins of the English People

*Poems*
Devouring Zodiac
The Choice
Phoenix and Unicorn
Air Journey

*Translations*
Ovid on Love
The Poems of François Villon (Everyman's Library)
Sappho of Lesbos

# THE REBEL KING

## The Story of Christ as Seen Against the Historical Conflict Between the Roman Empire and Judaism

by

Henry Marsh

COWARD, McCANN & GEOGHEGAN
NEW YORK

 Published on the same day in Canada by Longman Canada Limited, Toronto.

SBN: 698-10663-6
Library of Congress Catalog Card Number: 74-30594

PRINTED IN THE UNITED STATES OF AMERICA

# Preface

The events recorded in the New Testament must have seemed of little importance to any contemporary onlooker. A young man in a remote province of the Roman Empire had been executed for reasons that were not altogether clear and that were variously understood by various people.

To most of his fellow countrymen and certainly to those in authority among them he was a blasphemer who merited death for having arrogated to himself some of the rights and powers of the one true God. To the Roman officials of the province he appeared as a potential danger to the political stability of the regime. Perhaps he was seeking nothing more than some kind of harmless religious leadership. But there was a more sinister possibility. Was he aiming to become the head of an underground Jewish resistance movement which would defy the lawful government of Rome? In the past such militant movements had caused violent upheavals in the state, fostering armed uprisings which had been quelled only after the intervention of large armies. Or perhaps, again in defiance of Rome, he was advancing a claim to the kingship of the Jewish nation, over which Rome had set up her own chosen rulers whom it was politically expedient to defend.

But in any event, all these were purely provincial matters affecting only the stability of Judea. Once the execution was over, no one could have foreseen that the forces which the events generated would ultimately capture the imperial city itself and, through that city, all the lands of Rome's great empire.

These forces have held the attention of people, whether believers or unbelievers, for nearly two thousand years and radically changed the ethical, emotional, and intellectual attitudes of a great part of the human race. Despite the importance of the events, for many the drama is played on a dark stage, where the figures and actions of the protagonists are luminous, lit by a light which some consider divine and all must accept as dramatic. But the stage itself and the scenery and backcloth before which the drama was played lie in the darkness and are but dimly perceived.

This scene was, of course, Roman. The events took place within a land which, when Jesus was executed, had been occupied by Rome for some ninety years. It was a Roman official in a Roman court who imposed the death sentence; provincial auxiliaries of the Roman army performed the savage execution in the terrifying and unnatural darkness of Calvary. Later—and in vain—Roman troops kept guard before the entrance to the tomb. And before that appalling climax Jesus and his followers had worked within a system where Judea had its own Jewish rulers but where the brutal realities of power lay with the Roman authority.

Whether or not Jesus was divine, the historical and political background of his life merits detailed consideration. Those who accept him as God incarnate must surely accept the corollary that he chose to live his human life under the constraints of mortality and of the flesh. During his incarnation he was subjected to his social environment and to contemporary political pressures as much as any ordinary man. And it is by investigating that environment that tentative answers may be found to some of the many questions posed by the Gospels.

Why, at the time when Jesus was born and before he began his ministry, were the hopes of the Jewish people for the coming of their Messiah so high and so intense? What, to contemporary minds, both Jewish and Roman, did the word "Messiah" convey? Why, when John the Baptist began to call sinners to repentance, did people ask him, "Are you the Christ?" Why did Jesus so frequently use the metaphor or parable of a kingdom to describe the consummation of God's purpose? Why did he find it necessary to explain that the kingdom he had in mind was not of this world? Why was his followers' claim that he was the Son of God so acceptable not merely to his Jewish adherents (who might have some justification for this in their Messianic dreams) but also to the Gentile Christians in the Roman world? Why did the populace of Jerusalem, having hailed him as king on Palm Sunday, turn against him within four or five days, so that the same crowd called for his crucifixion on the following Friday and would not have their savage clamour brushed aside? Why did Jesus have to face trial three times? Within the orderly Roman Empire, where law was so elegantly organised, how did it happen that he came under the jurisdiction of three separate courts—that of the Sanhedrin, that of the tetrarch, Herod Antipas, and that of Pontius Pilate, the Roman prefect?

Having been found guilty of blasphemy by the Sanhedrin and having been taken before Pilate for sentence, why was the nature of his crime described on the gallows, not by the words "Here is Jesus of Nazareth, the blasphemer" but by the phrase "Here is Jesus of Nazareth, King of the Jews"? Over what other trials had Pilate presided, and how had he on earlier occasions solved the thorny problems presented by the stubborn Jewish people, so unbending in their religious beliefs and so resentful of their pagan and alien rulers?

Finally we shall consider what happened to the main protagonists of the drama after the Crucifixion. If the motive of Caiaphas in condemning Jesus was to remain in good standing with the Romans, how far was he successful in later years? If Pilate's motive was to appease the Jewish populace so as to maintain peace within his territory and so to advance his career, did the sacrifice he made of Jesus to this selfish cause bring him the success he hoped for? In fact his public career ended in disgrace.

These are some of the questions to which this book will propose tentative answers, derived from a study of the political situation in Judea before the birth of Jesus, during his lifetime, and immediately thereafter. The book is not an attempt to write a life of Jesus, but rather a brief description of the relationship between Rome and her puzzling subjects, the Jews. They were the heirs of an ancient kingdom which had reached its greatest splendour under the great King David and his son Solomon. But the kingdom had been destroyed by many invaders. Rome had partly revived it under Jewish rulers who were not descended from David and Solomon but who were the nominees of Rome itself.

Jesus was born in the reign of the first emperor, Augustus, and crucified in the reign of the second, Tiberius. For the folk dwelling in the hot plains and shady olive groves of Judea both emperors were remote figures living in a far city which few of them would ever see. But their power could be seen in the glittering figures of the troops quartered in Jerusalem, in Caesarea, and in other cities of their once-proud and now-vanquished kingom. Both emperors were semidivine; Augustus was the adopted son of Julius Caesar, who, after he died, had been declared a god by a solemn resolution of the Senate. Tiberius also had divine parentage, for he was the adopted son of Augustus, who in his turn was also deified by the Senate.

To the Romans the title of king was odious, and no emperor dared assume it. Julius Caesar had been assassinated on the mere suspicion that he had planned to establish a monarchy. To the Jews the title of king was a holy title, first bestowed by the prophet Samuel; and it had become the central theme of their memories of past glories and their hopes for future liberation.

It was inevitable that once Rome had entered Judea, the two cultures should clash and that many tensions should develop between them. The Roman officials, whether civil or military, had all at some time served in the army. They saw the maintenance of Rome's military power as their supreme duty. The Jews saw the maintenance of the law as theirs. All the Romans, from the governor down to the humblest private soldier, considered devotion to the emperor and to the state as the supreme loyalty. For the Jews the supreme loyalty was to their God, who had made a covenant with them and whose words, written on their sacred scroll, were kept in the innermost shrine of their ancient temple. This was the sombre background to the New Testament story. Dark was the scene, deep were the feelings of sorrow and hostility that filled the land. In such a theatre only a tragedy could be played.

At its lowest assessment, the story of Jesus is the recurrent story of how society destroys any man who seeks uncompromisingly to teach the truth without fear of authority or favour towards the influential. For Pythagoras the stake, for Socrates the cup of poison, and for Jesus the cross. A letter from Mara bar Saration, a Syrian, who was writing to his son shortly after A.D. 73 has survived.[1] He makes the same point, although it seems that he did not know the name of Jesus but merely that the Jews had once slain "their wise king." He points out that time and destiny avenge the murdered men. "What good did it do the Athenians to kill Socrates? . . . The Athenians died of famine. . . ." He also asks of what avail was it for the Jews to kill their king? And he adds, "Nor is the wise king dead: because of the new laws which he has given."

In this book I have tried not to take up any theological position, nor do I think it necessary to do so for the purposes which I have in mind. I have preferred to exclude such matters altogether so that each reader may take from the book the historical facts as presented, together with my own speculations, without there being any conflict between these and his own views.

H. M.

# Contents

# 1

# A Crowd of Gods

Rome did not, though this is what the world chiefly remembers, merely conquer the peoples of Europe, western Asia, and North Africa. To all the vanquished, whose culture and forms of government varied so widely, she taught her own ways and imposed on them her own pattern of society. Her invincible skill on the battlefield was matched by her dexterity in government. She did not uproot the barbarian institutions which she found in the conquered lands. Giving them new names, she reshaped them all, diverse as they were, to her single purpose. Traditional social structures—to which nations so stubbornly cling, ascribing to them the same sacred values as those of the freedom and independence of which they are alike the symbols and the defence—Rome adopted and brought persuasively within her own forms of government.

After the savagery of conquest there always followed the flattery of integration into and identification with the majestic splendour of the imperial state. Julius Caesar could massacre an entire tribe which had too gallantly withstood him. And he could cause his soldiers to strike off the right hands of all the men and boys of another, sending them bleeding away to ponder the bitter lesson of the legions' merciless invincibility. But later he gave Roman citizenship to all the Gauls. Nor did the conquered lose all their ancient rights and liberties by becoming a part of the larger imperial state. As in Gaul, so elsewhere. The tribal kingdoms of conquered Britain became recognised states in the Roman province. Their stockaded and primitive capitals, where kings and nobles dwelt in houses of clay and wattle, were resplendently rebuilt after the Roman fashion, with colonnaded marketplaces and bright temples. Gay theatres, rich with columns and marble seats, were built to the delight and pride of the new Romans who had so recently felt the weight of Roman arms. Kings and princes, local chieftains and tribal leaders sat in the assemblies which Rome organised, retaining their inherited pride and much of their old authority.

Nor was it only among the peoples of Europe that Rome transformed the barbarian societies which she had conquered. She achieved the same purpose among other and more alien people. In North Africa the great city of Leptis Magna stands to this day in the hot dry sunshine. Wide streets, neat shops, the theatre, forum, and port all bear witness to the skill with which Rome transplanted her ideas in faraway lands. In Turkey and

Syria, in Greece and Yugoslavia, in Britain and Spain, and in the ancient cities of Egypt the Roman genius brought together peoples and societies of widely different customs into a common culture.

Whatever might have been divisive, Rome adapted and reshaped as unifying forces. Tribal chiefs became Roman officers, proud to wear the crested helmets, bright breastplates, and pleated cloaks of the invincible master state. Former kings sat in local versions of the Senate. They became magistrates, gladly exchanging the style of king for the prouder titles of aedile or prefect, which they knew had been borne by the greatest of their conquerors.

So local loyalties were not destroyed, but transmuted from base barbarian metal into true imperial gold; and millions of people became citizens of Rome, through whose gates they had never entered, whose streets they had never trodden, and whose marble palaces and temples they would never see.

Religion, as the world is so often and so tragically reminded, can be among the most dividing of all social forces. But Rome succeeded in adapting even these to her purposes. She herself worshipped many gods, whose origins lay in her own tribal past. She was thus able to understand the wild gods of the Celts, Germans, and other barbarians. In them she recognised the primitive counterparts of her own divinities. Thus, the Romans mused, did we ourselves worship in the days of Romulus and of our own remotest ancestors. We too (as Ovid reminds us) once worshipped in the open fields, laying our offerings on rude altars of piled earth; our first theatre had heaped turfs for seats; and our gods were the savage gods (as are those of the barbarians today) of a younger, simpler, and more vigorous age.

So the barbarian gods were Rome's gods, still in their youth but nonetheless identifiable. Julius Caesar, in his account of his wars in Gaul, recorded that all the Gaulish nation was devoted to religion.[1] When faced by the perils of sickness or battle, they offered up victims to the gods, including human sacrifice. He found nothing strange in these customs or in their savage practice of burning men alive, crammed into huge wickerwork figures of the gods. On the contrary, he was able to identify their religion with that of Rome and to state that the Gauls chiefly worshipped the god Mercury. He did not merely compare their deity with the Roman god, but categorically stated that Mercury was the chief divinity of tribesmen who had probably never heard the god's name. Caesar added that they also worshipped Apollo, Mars, Jove, and Minerva and that they foretold the future by appeals to Dis, the god of the underworld. On the gods of Gaul, as on its people, he bestowed Roman citizenship. Just as their kings and chieftains were persuaded to sit in Roman assemblies, so were the divinities in their pantheon transported from the sacred groves of Gaul to the clouds of Olympus.

Caesar did the same for the Germans, telling us that they worshipped the sun and the moon and Vulcan.[2] Tacitus wrote that Mercury was the principal god of the German tribes and that they sacrificed vicitims to Mars and to Hercules.[3] He also reported that one German tribe, the Naharvali, worshipped the Roman immortals Castor and Pollux, in an ancient grove.[4] In his *Annals* he saw Hercules as a native of Egypt, no doubt equating the god of some local cult with the classical hero.[5]

Rome did not merely identify these foreign deities with her own divinities. Not content with her own gods and goddesses whom her people had worshipped from time immemorial, she adopted the gods of many of the conquered people. Jove, whose temple stood on the Capitoline Hill, was the ancient tutelary deity of their city and empire and his eagles led them into war. Mars inspired the legions. Juno presided over the decorum of marriage and the dignity of matrons. Vesta, virgin goddess of fire, was particularly sacred, as were her virgin priestesses. Now to these and to her other native gods alien deities were added. Some Romans worshipped Isis, who had come to the city from Egypt. Others followed the cult of Cybele, castrating themselves in ecstasies of masochistic devotion. The soldiers adopted the religion of their Persian adversaries and took to their hearts Mithras, the Lord of Light, with his handsome face and Phrygian cap. Wherever there was a garrison his statue was set up, usually depicted in the act of slaying a bull, for it was in a bull's blood that his followers were baptised.

So gods and goddesses, both native and alien, abounded among the Romans, and their images were everywhere to be seen. Every household had its *larium,* a simple domestic shrine where figurines of gods and goddesses were placed. For the rich these might be in silver or in bronze, while even the poorest could afford the mass-produced pipe-clay statuettes whose fragments are so frequently found on many Roman archaeological sites.

So to the Romans it was natural for a man to hold many gods in affection and for artists to make images of the deities for private shrine and public temple. And almost all the nations they encountered had similar practices which Rome could easily comprehend.

But there was one people whose religion Rome was never able to understand. These were the Jews, dwelling in and around the ancient city of Jerusalem, whose territory had been taken by a Roman army under Pompey in 63 B.C. Rome never truly assimilated them, although they had far more in common with the Roman world than had the barbarian races of Europe, whom Rome found it so easy to bring within the confines of her empire and the patterns of her society.

Like the Romans, the Jews boasted a long, honourable, and well-documented history. Like the Romans, they rigidly followed a set of written laws, possessed a body of ancient poetry, and proudly remembered the names of their kings of long ago and the triumphs of ancient victories. Like the Romans, they built enduringly in stone; and the centre of their worship was no grove of trees or circle of rough-hewn monoliths, but a magnificent temple which Rome herself might have been proud to have erected.

When it came to religion, the Romans celebrated festivals whose origins lay in their remote past but whose symbolism was still fresh and meaningful. Such was the Lupercalia, the wolf festival held each February, when naked men ran through the city streets, whipping the passersby with raw and bleeding strips of animal skin; such too the Saturnalia of December, when the feast of the midwinter equinox was riotously enjoyed. So it was with the Jews. They celebrated the old feast of the Passover at the time of the spring equinox, eating the sacrificial paschal lamb in a ritual feast; and they celebrated their New Year with wine, prayer, and candlelight.

So all in all, when Rome first entered Jerusalem, it might have been predicted that she would assimilate this literate, religious, and highly civilised people more easily than the ferocious and untutored tribes of Europe. But behind the superficial similarities there was one fundamental difference: The Romans worshipped many gods and the Jews but one.

This the Romans found quite bewildering. Even more incomprehensible was the fact that the Jews set up no statues and created no pictures wherein to show the face and figure of their one God. Depictions of deities were, for the Romans, not only a natural but an essential part of all religions.

When Pompey stormed Jerusalem, he visited the Temple and went into the Holy of Holies—the innermost shrine which only the high priest might enter to perform the annual rites on the Day of Atonement. There, surely, he would find some most sacred and ancient statue. But in the curtained chamber he found nothing but a gold-decked wooden chest in which were stored copies of the books which the Jews held sacred. By these books and by the law which they embodied—the Torah—they lived and organised their society. But to a Roman a shrine without a visible godhead was a strange and unnatural sight. Rome's total failure to understand the Jews, which lasted for a hundred and fifty years, seems to have begun in that empty shrine, with the proud and armoured figure of Pompey gazing in bewilderment at that empty room, bereft of any statue of the vanquished people's God.[6]

This bewilderment forever underlay Rome's relations with the Jews, her policies in Judea, her handling of the Jesus affair, and her treatment of the new faith which developed after his death. It had two savage and bloody outcomes: first, the total destruction of Jerusalem by a Roman army under Titus in A.D. 70; second, the cruel persecutions of the early Christians.

Yet the strange and invisible God whom Rome could not understand finally captured both the city and the empire. As redefined and explained by Jesus, he came to be worshipped by emperor, citizen, and barbarian. The crowd of ancient gods gave way before him; Jove, Mithras, Isis, Cybele, and the rest now lie in the shadows; and over them the strange God of the Jews and his puzzling exponent, Jesus, finally triumphed.

# 2

# Judea—the Roman Province

All the details of the Jewish faith were recorded in their sacred books and were available to any Roman willing to study Hebrew or to question Jewish leaders and teachers. But the evidence was for the most part not studied, nor were the facts obtained. References to the Jewish faith in Latin literature largely consist of allusions to the strange customs to which it led. The poet Juvenal wrote of their practice of refraining from all activity on every seventh day.[1] Pliny refers to the contumely which the Jews felt for any depiction of their god.[2] Others saw them as mere fortune-tellers and soothsayers.

The poet Horace made them a symbol for superstitious credulity.[3] Describing a journey he made with a friend from Rome to Brindisi, he records a tale of magic which they heard on the way. There was an altar on which, according to local folk, incense would melt of its own accord, without the need for any fire. "A circumcised Jew," exclaims Horace, "may believe such things. I shall not!" The word he uses for "circumcised," *apella,* is contemptuous and slightly bawdy. It means literally "the skinless one."

In another poem Horace mocks the Jews with further bawdry.[4] He is plagued by a talkative friend whose chatter never stops. Desperately Horace points out that "today is the thirtieth Sabbath," implying that on such a day even his friend's tongue should take a rest. "Or," he adds, "do you want the Jews to break wind against you?" Persius, the satirical poet, also derides "the circumcised Sabbath" of the Jews.[5]

From all these and similar remarks by Rome's more gossipy writers several facts emerge. First, the number of Jews in Rome was large enough for them to have become notorious. Second, the average educated Roman saw them as a ridiculous and superstitious sect, ready to believe in local miracles and tales like that of the magic altar. Next, all the world knew and found it a matter of ribald comment that they followed the extraordinary practice of mutilation by circumcision. It was also common knowledge that they ceased from every kind of activity every seventh day—apparently for no more compelling reason than ancient superstition. They were fit objects for scorn, derision, and contempt.

One writer at least approached the topic with more gravity. Tacitus attempted a serious description of the Jewish people and their faith.[6] As we should expect from such a careful writer, his account is accurate as to essentials, but his hostility to the Jews is apparent. His attitude may be taken as typical of that of an educated Roman and therefore of the imperial officials and magistrates who administered the new province. It was made up of considerable knowledge, a total lack of appreciation of the merits of the Jewish faith, and an unshakeable view that the Jewish nation was obstinate and perverse, holding all civilised practices in contempt and stubbornly pursuing outlandish customs that were utterly abhorrent by all normal standards. Such, then, might well have been the views of Pontius Pilate, the Roman official who played such an important role in the drama of Jesus some forty years before Tacitus was writing.

Tacitus, after improbably placing the origins of the Jews in Crete, writes of their sojourn in Egypt, but as masters not as slaves. He speaks of "a pestilential disease" (perhaps an echo of the biblical plagues of Egypt) which moved the local king to exterminate them as being a people "detested by the gods." They gathered around their leader, Moses, who ordered them to seek no help "from gods or men" but to put their trust in him. And he led them out of Egypt across a desert.

So far Tacitus is following the biblical account fairly closely. But he now introduces a new incident. The Old Testament tells us how, when their water failed in the desert, "they came to Elim, where were twelve wells of water, and three score and ten palm trees." (Exodus 15:27). But according to Tacitus, Moses found the oasis by following a herd of wild asses. They led him to an oasis where grasses grew and where he found plentiful supplies of water. There is a certain logic and probability in this addition. What better way to find water in the wilderness than to follow a herd of animals to their drinking place? The use to which Tacitus puts the story is interesting, for he alleges that to commemorate the affair, the Jews kept a statue of an ass in the sanctuary of their temple. His tone is contemptuous, for the ass was, with the Romans as with us, a symbol of all that is stupid, stubborn, and ridiculous. The story became firmly attached to Rome's beliefs about Jews and Christians. We shall meet an echo of the tale later when we come to see a crude and derisory drawing of a crucified man with a long-eared ass' head. And if Tacitus is recording a widely held belief, then many Roman eyebrows would have been raised when they heard the news of Jesus' entry into Jerusalem riding on an ass. The whole noisy and troublesome episode was clearly connected with the mob's bewildering and distasteful religion and therefore to be mistrusted and watched with considerable care.

Distasteful the religion certainly was. Tacitus expressed his disgust with epigrammatic brevity: "Whatever is sacred to the Romans is unholy to the Jews; and whatever is unlawful and impious among other folk is for them righteous."[7] He lists their impieties. The ram, sacred to Jupiter Ammon, they slaughtered as a sacrifice. (Was this perhaps a reference to the Passover lamb?) The ox, worshipped as the god Apis in Egypt, suffered a like fate at their hands. The pig (and no doubt Tacitus remembered that this animal had, since prehistoric times, been sacred to Ceres and Demeter) they would not eat. All the nations of the world added yeast to their wheat flour, but the Jews perversely ate unleavened bread. They insisted upon the uncouth rite of circumcision, and "all who join their religion must undergo that operation." Tacitus described their close-built society in hostile terms: They showed compassion to one another but total hatred to all others. They abjured all contact with women other than those of their own race.

Tacitus adds that the first thing which converts to the Jewish faith were taught was "to hold the gods in contempt." The fervour of their monotheism seemed to the Romans to be very close to atheism. To deny the existence of the ancient deities was a sacrilege which could not be redeemed by their eccentric worship of their own mysterious divinity.

He contrasted them with the Egyptians, with whom superficially they seemed to have so much in common. Like the Egyptians, they did not cremate their dead, as did the Romans and so many other nations, but buried them. Like the Egyptians, they believed in an afterlife. But according to Tacitus, the similarities stopped there. The Egyptians worshipped numerous animals and images, all made by the hand of man and all received by them as gods. But the Jews "acknowledge one God only, and conceive of him by the mind alone, condemning as impious all who, with perishable materials, wrought into the human shape any representations of the deity." Clearly it was this lack of a visible focus of worship that puzzled and indeed offended him more than the mere conception of one God. He went on: "That being, they say, is above all and everlasting, neither susceptible of likeness nor subject to decay."

This was a good and accurate description of the

Jewish God, for he was from everlasting to everlasting and, unlike all mortal things, was unblemished by the rust of time. Note too that Tacitus, in spite of his hostility, had an understanding of the repugnance felt by the Jews for the depiction of their God. Because he was conceived "by the mind alone" and because he was not "subject to decay," it was utterly wrong to project physically what was a mental or spiritual conception or to portray in perishable materials that which was eternal and everlasting.

However, one of the consequences of the Jewish refusal to accept images of God struck Tacitus as politically unfortunate, if not actually subversive. They carried their ban on images beyond the depiction merely of the divinity. Because of their strict interpretation of the Second Commandment, the Jews made no statues of men. "In this way," wrote Tacitus, "they do not flatter their kings, nor show their respect for the Caesars." To the Roman mind this was totally unacceptable.

The greatest honour one could do to a living man was to set up his statue. From time to time the grateful Senate voted to emperors the right to set up statues of themselves—usually outside Italy. Before every legion there was borne not only its standard, the rallying point in times of battle, the symbol of the legion's soul, a sacred and venerated object; in addition, special officers clad in leopard skin carried aloft portraits of the reigning Caesar, both to do him honour and to express their loyalty to Rome and the state. Every other nation within the empire accepted these practices and further accepted that the emperor was partly divine and that outside Rome itself he was the tutelary deity of the empire. On the altars set up in the provinces "to Rome and Augustus" no provincials hesitated to burn their incense as a mark of loyalty and respect. Not so the Jews. Their strict monotheism and that of their successors, the Christians, prevented any recognition of the emperor's divine status. Many Christians, as heirs to the Jewish tradition, were to suffer death for refusing what to the Romans was a courteous and patriotic gesture with no spiritual significance—the sprinkling of a little incense on these altars. This was yet another sign of the contumacious obduracy of the Jewish people.

Once Judea had become a Roman possession, how was one to govern such a strange people? Before the conquest the Jews had been governed by kings and by a religious council presided over by the high priest. Recognising the thorny problems involved in ruling such an obstinate and turbulent people, Rome destroyed neither institution. She frequently retained native kings in this way in many of her territories. There were such monarchs both in Syria and Cappadocia. A similar king reigned in Britain. Tacitus records how, under Britain's first Roman governor, certain districts were bestowed upon Cogidumnus, a British king, who reigned with great loyalty to Rome up to Tacitus' own times.[8] He adds the bitter comment that "this was done in accordance with the ancient and well-established Roman practice of making even kings the instrument of servitude." There is in Chichester, England, an inscribed stone on which Cogidumnus is described not only as king but as the emperor's imperial delegate, a title no doubt bestowed both to flatter him and to buy his loyalty. The ruins of his great palace at Fishbourne stand to this day, evidence of Rome's more substantial and glittering bribe.

Rome followed the same practice in Judea. Following Julius Caesar's assassination, Mark Antony and Augustus confirmed Herod on the throne of Judea in 40 B.C. Herod was not welcomed by the Jewish people, who backed Antigonus, a prince of the ancient Hasmonean dynasty. It was only after a long and bitter struggle that he secured Jerusalem and his kingdom. Herod had picked his way warily through the tangles of friendships and enmities which blossomed and withered with such bewildering speed in the turbulent days of his youth. He had been a friend of men whose names were to be immortal. The great Julius had befriended him. Mark Antony had been a friend and a supporter. Cleopatra had used all her artifices and stratagems, of which she was a consummate mistress, to seduce him into an illicit intercourse with her.[9] He had been crafty enough to ensure that, after her death and Antony's defeat, he won the friendship of Antony's onetime enemy, Augustus Caesar. Assassination, civil war, the clash of personalities in the council chamber and of armed legions on many a bloody field had left his position unchanged and unchallenged. He was one of the great contrivers and survivors of history.

He was a loyal servant of Rome, sending troops to assist an imperial campaign in Arabia in 25 B.C. He was rewarded by an enlargement of his realm. Apart from his royal revenues, Herod was a wealthy man in his own right. He devoted much of his wealth to erecting great buildings in his kingdom and, to please his Roman masters, elsewhere in the empire. It was not without offence to his own people that he built, at his own expense, fine temples to the pagan gods outside his own land both in Athens and Sparta.

In Jerusalem itself he restored and beautified the Temple, surrounding it with a colonnade and creating massive gateways. When Jesus debated in the Temple as a boy and when as a man he angrily cleansed it of the moneylenders, we must remember that the setting was bright and new, with the freshly hewn stone glistening in the hot sunshine and the pillars of the new colonnade casting their slender shadows across the courtyard.

To the northwest of the Temple he rebuilt an ancient fortress and named it the Antonia, after his friend and patron, the gay Mark Antony. It was in this stern fortress that part of the final tragedy of Jesus was played out. For here the soldiers lodged and thither Jesus was taken on his way to his final suffering. Antony, never an emperor, was the ancestor of many, including Nero. It was a strange chance that brought Jesus to the grim and forbidding barracks, named after the ancestor of emperors who were so cruelly to persecute and torture his followers in the years to come.

As we have seen, Tacitus had not failed to observe that the British king, Cogidumnus, was a traitor to his people, used by the Roman authorities as an instrument of enslavement. How much more readily did Herod's subjects see him as no true king of theirs, but a tool of the occupying power? His record of building temples to pagan gods overseas was a blasphemy not to be redeemed by his restoration of the Temple in Jerusalem. And even in rebuilding the Temple he had affronted the people and God himself. For over it he had set up a huge gilt eagle as a gesture of loyalty to Rome. This was a twofold insult to his people: It identified their king with the tyrannous might of the occupying power, the insignia of whose imperial power had always been Jove's predatory eagles; second, it was a quite appalling defiance of the Second Commandment, and to introduce such a graven image into the sacred precincts of the Temple was a grievous wrong both to the Jewish people and to their God.

For all his power and wealth, Herod's life was made tragic by his sense of insecurity, his willingness to commit the bloodiest of crimes to maintain his doubtful position of king, and his glowering mistrust of all around him. He divorced his first wife, by whom he had a son named Antipater, in order to wed Mariamne, who was a princess of the legitimate Hasmonean royal family—no doubt intending thereby to buttress his claim to be the legitimate king. But, as Josephus tells us, he later had Mariamne executed in a fit of jealousy, urged on by his sister Salome. His two sons by her were also executed when they grew to manhood, since they, through their mother, had a better claim to the Jewish crown than he himself. Thereafter he made Antipater his heir and coregent—only to fall into a fit of suspicion of him and so stripped him of power and drove him from his court.

A like fate befell others of his sons. He could brook no equal or any successor but lived in continuous and paranoid apprehension. In later ages he became the archetype of the bloody and ruthless tyrant. It was fear that drove him on, insecurity that made him shed so much blood, and the knowledge that he had betrayed his people and his God that made him the wretched and unhappy murderer whom the world so scornfully remembers.

# 3

# The Old Kingdom and the New

From the earliest times the Jewish nation, as yet no more than a nomadic tribe of herdsmen and tent dwellers, was ruled by patriarchs. These were the fathers of their people over whom they held unquestioned sway. Later, as their society became more complex, they came to be governed by magistrates whom they called judges. These were selected by the acclaim of the elders or marked out by some special sign from Israel's God. The greatest, as well as the last, of these judges was Samuel, who played a significant part in strengthening the tradition, so dominant in Jewish history, that a leader derived his authority from a special relationship with God. Like Moses, he had spent his life in close and direct colloquy with the Creator. It was through men of this stamp that the God of Israel revealed to his people his will and purpose.

During his magistracy, Israel, no longer a nomadic tribe but a settled nation with territories to defend, was beset by many foes. She spent long years of strenuous war, fending off the aggression of neighbouring tribes. The nation suffered numerous defeats, the most disastrous of which involved the humiliating loss of the Ark of the Covenant. This was the ancient chest in which were stored the stone tablets of the law, delivered to Moses by the awful hand of God himself. This holy relic was the symbol of Jewish independence, containing a divine guarantee of their continued existence as a nation, in the form of the compact made between them and their all-powerful God.

Their enemies, the Philistines, placed the Ark in the temple of their god Dagon. But the image of Dagon fell and was shattered. Wherever the Philistines took the Ark disaster befell them. Nevertheless, they held it for more than twenty years, and the people of Israel were long bereft of their most sacred possession. Samuel told them that this deprivation was a sign of God's wrath, for they had begun to worship false gods. They accepted the warning: "Then the children of Israel did put away Baalim and Ashtaroth, and serve the Lord only" (I Samuel 7:4). The next time the Philistines attacked, "the Lord thundered with a great thunder upon the Philistines, and discomfited them; they were smitten before Israel."

When Samuel grew old, the people became anxious as to who would head them in war and worship as he had done. The elders asked him not to appoint his sons to be judges after him, but to give them a king. Their wars with neighbouring nations, who were ruled by kings, had taught them that a warlike monarch was the most effective leader of a nation in arms. The supreme power of a king bestowed power upon his people. His valour inspired, and his sword and his chariots protected them. The victorious empires they had encountered had all been led by kings. After a generation of humiliating defeat it was expedient that they too should adopt this martial form of government.

The conception of the kingdom was to have enormous influence on future events, and succeeding generations clung tenaciously to the idea of its revival. Yet Samuel resisted the idea, and the kingdom was founded against the express will of God.

For God ordered Samuel to tell the people that, in demanding a king, they had forsaken him and to warn them what manner of man a king might be. So he told the elders that to create a king would be to set up a tyrant. A king would call out their sons to be his charioteers and horsemen. Young men of Israel would be forced to run before the king's chariot like slaves. Free men would have to plough the king's fields, to reap his harvest, to labour at forge and anvil to make his weapons of war and the costly trappings of his chariots. A king would take their daughters to cook for him and to bake his bread. He could seize their fields and vineyards to give to his favourites and would impose heavy taxes.

But the people persisted, and Samuel reluctantly appointed Saul to be king over them. His manner of consecrating Saul to regality was thus: "Then Samuel took a vial of oil and poured it upon his head, and kissed him, and said, 'Is it not because the Lord hath anointed thee to be captain over his inheritance?'" (I Samuel 10:1). Note that the kingship was a military one, for Saul was appointed expressly to be a captain, a war leader. Note too the anointing with oil, which became an indispensable part of the ritual of creating kings and is still practised in the twentieth century during the coronation ceremony of English kings and queens.

To the Jews the titles of "King" and "the Anointed One" were completely interchangeable. After the precedent set by Samuel it was always the anointing with oil which bestowed on a man both royalty and the magic of kingship. Whatever other pomp might attend on a king's enthronement was only to glorify the occasion and did not contribute in any way to the validity of the anointing rites. The gleaming helmet of a warrior king, the costly breastplate and jewelled rings, the brazen sound of trumpets that went before him, the obedience of his captains, the gold and silver heaped in his treasure house—all these were signs that he was set apart from other men. But they symbolised and did not create his royalty. That was done by the vial of oil, the touch of which invested him with a share of the divine authority.

The Hebrew word "to anoint" was *mashah,* and "the Anointed One" was the *Mashih* or, as brought into European languages by translations of the Bible made in the sixteenth century, the Messiah. It was the king's most precious, as well as his most usual, title.

The reign of Saul, Israel's first Anointed One, was largely occupied with war. Nor at first were the people disappointed that a king would lead them victoriously. Saul was tall and powerful, and there was "none like him among all the people" (I Samuel 10:24). He liberated the city of Jabesh-gilead from the Ammonites. His son Jonathan defeated the Philistines in Geba. But his reign ended in disaster, for to the distress of the ageing Samuel, the people began to desert their God, who rejected Saul and ordered Samuel to set matters right.

Seeking a successor to Saul, Samuel sent the great ones of the nation, including Jesse. But God told him to reject Jesse and the seven sons he had brought with him. Samuel asked whether these were all the children he had. And Jesse said, "There remains the youngest, behold , he keepeth the sheep." So Samuel sent for the boy, who was named David, and found him to be handsome and of a commanding presence. And God instructed him to anoint David as the future king, and Saul made David his armour bearer. But David was not only a man of war but a musician. And "when the evil spirit from God was upon Saul . . . David took an harp and played with his hand; and Saul was refreshed and was well, and the evil spirit departed from him" (I Samuel 16:23). This was the man—king, warrior, religious leader, poet, and musician—who was the ancestor of Jesus.

The attachment of David to Saul's son Jonathan is well known. Later, when Saul tried to kill David, it was Jonathan who prevented it.

In the first battle against the Philistines, Jonathan was slain and Saul himself sorely wounded by an enemy bowman. His spirit broken by defeat and by the loss of his son, and finding that his wounds were bringing death but tardily to him, he thrust himself through with his own sword. So perished in defeat and despair the first *Mashih*—or Anointed One—of Israel.

David succeeded to the kingdom and polished the rough-cut gem of monarchy to a new and enduring brightness. He was forever remembered as one of the greatest leaders the Jews had ever known. Triumphant in war, just in peace, a true follower of his nation's God, his reign was the high noon of the kingdom's prosperity. He flourished towards the end of the eleventh century B.C., about a thousand years before Rome seized Judea. A thousand years is not too long for a great man to be remembered or for a nation to honour his descendants. King Alfred of Wessex died about a thousand years ago, and his descendants still sit on the throne of England by right of that descent. So it was with David. As Alfred stamped his personality and virtues indelibly on the English monarchy, so did David on the kingdom of Israel. During his reign of some forty years he scattered his nation's enemies and made the kingdom of Judea supreme throughout Israel. He built a new capital for the nation at Jerusalem on Mount Zion, the site of an ancient fortress. The Ark of the Covenant, now triumphantly recovered from Israel's foes, was there set up, and Jerusalem became a holy place. He captured from his enemies great treasures of gold and silver, all of which he dedicated to God's service.

He was not without sin. He lay with Bathsheba, a married woman of great beauty, abusing his royal power to command her to be brought to him for his pleasure. He arranged by trickery for her husband to be slain in battle, adding the sin of murder to the sin of adultery; but neither sin was counted against him by his adoring people. Some of his sons also followed unrighteousness. One, Ammon, fell sick of love for his own sister Tamar and raped her. Absolom, another of David's sons, arranged for Ammon to be murdered. He rebelled against David, who was forced to flee Jerusalem.

So David's reign contained much sorrow and turmoil. But it was only its prosperity and piety that were remembered. And its brightness was a star guiding and comforting the Jewish people through all the disasters which befell them from generation to generation.

Many were the vicissitudes suffered by the kingdom which Saul had founded and which David had glorified. More than once foreign conquerors strode insolently through the cities and farmlands of Judea. Alien tyrants ruled over the Jewish people, and their God was derided. But though the kingdom was to be finally overthrown, there remained inviolate an invisible kingdom, made up of their memories of ancient glories and the sure hope that these would in due time be renewed. Within the invisible kingdom there lay unwavering worship of the true God, compassion, and the knowledge of God's promised protection. To comfort themselves the Jewish people looked forward to the fortunate and peaceful times when a prince of David's house would again rule them and when once more they would have a true king, an Anointed One, the Messiah.

The dream was vividly expressed by the prophet

Isaiah, who lived between 750 and 600 B.C. and in whose days the Jewish nation was woefully beset. Hostile armies were marching against them. War, invasion, and defeat were once more shattering the kingdom. Isaiah saw these sorrows as God's punishment for the people's sinful ways. The rituals of burnt offerings and of sacrifice were faithfully performed. But the true spirit of worship had vanished. "Learn to do well," Isaiah exhorted. "Seek judgement, relieve the oppressed, judge the fatherless, plead for the widow." Jerusalem was no longer the seat of righteousness. Silver had become dross and the good wine of religion had been watered down. Men were deserting the faith; women were seeking after necklaces, jewellery, and fine clothes.

At this time the powerful states of Egypt, Babylon, and Syria menaced the visible realm, just as unrighteousness threatened the invisible kingdom. But Isaiah comforted his people with the promises of the restoration of the kingdom. "As birds flying, so will the Lord of Hosts defend Jerusalem; defending also he will deliver it; and passing over he will preserve it" (Isaiah 31:5).

In another passage he specifically foretold the coming of a just and pious king, an Anointed One, who would restore the ancient values and prosperity of the kingdom:

> For unto us a child is born, unto us a son is given; and the government shall be upon his shoulder and his name shall be called Wonderful Counsellor, the Mighty

> God, the Father, the Prince of Peace. Of the increase of his government and peace there shall be no end, upon the throne of David and upon his kingdom, to order it and to establish it with judgement and with justice from henceforth even for ever (Isaiah 9:6).

Isaiah's words specifically identify the throne of the Messiah with the throne of David, and the latter's reign is now clearly recorded as a golden age, to the restoration of which the whole nation looked forward with a deep longing.

His words contained a vastly more important implication. The great kings of the past, including David, had ruled with God's authority and had interpreted his will in the fashion and purposes of their government. Now by his words Isaiah extended the authority of the expected king who would not govern merely in the name of God; he himself would be called the Mighty One, the Everlasting Father. This identification of the expected Messiah with the one and eternal God contained a completely new conception of man's relationship with the deity. God, not through the instrument of a chosen king or of a prophet with whom he held a special relationship, would himself one day govern the kingdom and sit on the throne of David. For future generations this could mean only one of two things: Either the simplistic conception of one God was to be modified, since God himself would take the form of an earthly king, or God himself in his proper person would appear on earth as a wonderful counsellor, sitting on the throne of David. These were revolutionary ideas—a far cry from the conception of God as a spirit and a preparation for the belief that God himself could visit the mortal world.

When Isaiah was writing, the kingdom was in being and a king still sat on the throne. Isaiah's life extended over three reigns. What, one wonders, did they make of his prophecy that greater and wiser than the kings would one day sit on the throne which they occupied? Such a prophecy must have appeared as a criticism of their own competence and piety. But perhaps men were already distinguishing between the visible and the invisible kingdom—between the earthly affairs of the Jewish people and their special relationship with their Creator, who was, as it were, an overlord of their kings.

In another passage Isaiah added another significant component to the growing story of the Messiah. Ahaz, a prince of the house of Judea, was awaiting an attack on Jerusalem by a combined army of two hostile kings. Greatly troubled, he was comforted by Isaiah with the prophecy that the power of his enemies would be broken. God then spoke directly to Ahaz, suggesting that he should ask for a sign. But Ahaz declined, saying that he would not so put God to the test:

> . . . Hear ye now, O house of David; Is it a small thing for you to weary men, but will ye weary my God also?
>
> Therefore the Lord himself shall give you a sign; Behold, a virgin shall conceive, and bear a son, and shall call his name Immanuel (Isaiah 7:13–14).

This statement that, as one of the signs God would give

of the fulfillment of his promise, a virgin would conceive and bear a son was to have a profound effect some six or seven centuries later.

The statement, of course, comes from a passage written in highly symbolic language. In foretelling the defeat of the enemies of the house of David, we are told of "the flight that is in the uttermost part of the rivers of Egypt" and of "the bee that is in the land of Assyria." We are told of the desolate valleys and the holes of the rocks into which they shall come. We are told how the Lord will "shave with a razor that is hired" and of the briars and thorns that will grow where once stood a thousand vines. All these phrases are clearly used as images of the essential message and must be so interpreted. But later ages took the statement about a virgin birth (which could perhaps be as symbolic as the rest) as literal truth.

Two other aspects of this prophecy were also important: First, it was addressed to a prince of the house of David; second, it was linked with God's assurance that the power of the enemies of the house of David would be totally destroyed.

Micah, a younger contemporary of Isaiah, also foretold the coming of the Anointed One, a new ruler in Israel. Like Isaiah, he stressed the peace which such a ruler would bring. But he went further and foretold in detail whence this Messiah would come:

> But thou, Bethlehem Ephratah, though thou be little among the thousands of Judah, yet out of thee shall he come forth unto me that is to be ruler in Israel; whose

> goings forth have been from of old, from everlasting. . . .
>
> And he shall stand and feed in the strength of the Lord, in the majesty of the name of the Lord his God; and they shall abide; for now shall he be great unto the ends of the earth.
>
> And this man shall be the peace . . . (Micah 5:2 and 4).

King David himself had been born in Bethlehem of Judea. So the further mention by Micah of Bethlehem represented, as did the words of Isaiah, the close identification of the expected king with the royal house of the great David.

The psychological motives which drove the Jews to seek comfort in a remembrance of past glories and the hope of the latter's restoration are not unique in history. Many nations in defeat or under foreign occupation retain dreams of their former kings. In the Middle Ages Arthur was seen as *rex quondam et rex futurus*—the king that was and was to be. Men said that he would come again whenever his island of Britain was in mortal peril. On the continent there were legends of armed champions who lay sleeping in a deep cavern and who would rouse themselves whenever Christendom was in danger. In India to this day the Parsees (descendants of refugees who fled from Persia centuries ago) still keep their calendar by the years of the reign of their last king, Yazdezard Sheryar, who has been dead these thirteen hundred years. Neither the destruction of their kingdom nor the death of their king is recognised. Yazdezard still nominally reigns, though he is now but scattered dust, and, by implication, he may one day come again.

So the Jewish people foresaw the coming of a new king who would rebuild their ancient glories.

Isaiah gave to the dream the substance of words seven hundred years before the birth of Jesus. The dream was renewed from generation to generation, becoming more intense whenever the Jewish people suffered defeat or disaster. It endured for more than a thousand years and spilled over into the world of Greece and Rome. It has been said that during the reign of Augustus (who was emperor at the time of the birth of Jesus) the oracle at Delphi had predicted that a Jewish boy *(Hebraeus puer)* would rule over all the earth.[1]

There is much firmer evidence for the dream's revival a century or so later. Vespasian, then no more than a successful legionary commander, decided to make a bid for the imperial diadem (in A.D. 69). His biographer recorded that he was encouraged to risk all on an armed uprising, any failure in which would have meant his degradation and death, by a rumour that was then rife that a man should come out of the East who would rule the world. He himself held command in Syria and he felt that this applied to him. The episode shows the Messianic hope still persisting in and near Syria half a century and more after the Crucifixion.

Long before this, with what appeared to be the final destruction of their independence by the Roman power, it was but natural for the Jewish people to renew their old dream. Indeed, whenever their fortunes were at low ebb, the compensatory dream of the restored kingdom came most vividly into their minds. So that with the extension of Rome's military power into their territory, the smouldering hopes of the coming of a new king burst into flame. And the dream had now taken a definite shape in the writings of the prophets.

Prophets, as the Greek root of the word implies, were originally orators and spokesmen. Men of divinely inspired eloquence, they gave voice to the will of God, exhorting the people to virtue. Later their exhortations were seen as predictions of the time when men would return to virtue and their rebukes as portents of the disasters that would follow sin. So their words came to be interpreted as prophecies in the modern sense—clear predictions of future events—and later ages searched for their literal fulfilment. In the light of this newer concept of prophecy, men now knew with some precision the conditions which the new king would fulfil. He would be born in a village called Bethlehem in the province of Ephraim. He would be born of a virgin. He would be a descendant of David. He would be not only the Wise Counsellor and the Prince of Peace but would himself be the Mighty One, the Father.

# 4

# The Infant King

The last years of King Herod's troubled reign brought increasing unhappiness to his people. Immediately after his death the elders of his kingdom made the long journey to Rome and petitioned Augustus Caesar not to appoint any member of Herod's family as king. For them to have preferred the rule of an alien and pagan emperor to government by a Jewish king, their disgust for Herod must have been extreme indeed. And for the delegation to have left so speedily for the distant capital, the sense of oppression and the spirit of unrest must already have been growing in men's hearts long before King Herod's death.

Rumours began to spread that the promised king of the house of David would soon be born, to rule in peace over a reunited, prosperous, and pious nation. The hopes on which these rumours were based did not have merely a religious or mystical foundation. Men, sickened by the cruelties of a puppet king and by the arrogance of the foreign power which supported him, longed for the reestablishment of the visible and physical kingdom of former days. Many centuries had passed since David, son of Jesse the Bethlehemite, had been sought out by Samuel, who had journeyed to Bethlehem to find him (I Samuel 16:2 and 4). But David's descendants still dwelt in the land.

In a society whose origins were patriarchal and where all men counted their descent from one of the sons of Israel, genealogies were kept and members of David's house were known and recognised. In Nazareth in Galilee, for example, there lived a man named Joseph who could trace back his descent from David through thirteen generations (Matthew 1:17). As the people's sorrows heightened their dreams and hopes for a renewal of the kingdom, many members of the house of David must have wondered whether they or their children were destined to play any royal part in the dream's fulfilment. If so, it is most unlikely that Joseph was one of them. He had only recently become engaged to a girl called Mary. No doubt he looked forward to the time when he and Mary would have children, but since he lived in Nazareth, it was there that any sons of theirs would be born. None of them could be the hoped-for king of Micah's prophecy, which specifically foretold that the Messiah was to be born, like David, in a town named Bethlehem.

There was another and more distressing reason. Shortly after his espousal he found that Mary was already pregnant. We can imagine the sorrow this caused him. Indeed Matthew (1:19) reports that Joseph considered divorcing her. A compassionate man, he would have done this privately so as not to make a public example of her. Thus, while the rumours of the new king spread throughout Judea and beyond, Joseph had more personal matters to think of.

Then two events occurred. First, and again the authority is Matthew (1:20), Joseph had a dream in which he was visited by a messenger from God who hailed him as "son of David." This reminder of his royal descent was followed by an exhortation not to reject Mary. The child whom she was carrying had been conceived in her by the spirit of God. Joseph awakened from his dream and henceforward accepted Mary as his wife. Thus was fulfilled, according to Matthew, the prophecy made to Ahaz that a virgin should bear a son. But, contrary to the prophecy, when the child was born, Mary and Joseph called him not Immanuel but Jesus.

Luke (1:34) has a different version, in which God's messenger appeared to the incredulous Mary—"How shall this be, seeing I know not a man?"—to announce that she would bear a son to whom the Lord would give "the throne of his father David." Then, as if to confirm the news of the dream and the vision, there took place the second event.

This was directly connected with the Roman occupation and Roman methods of government and was the first episode in the story on which the Roman power exercised a direct influence. Cyrenius, governor of Syria, announced that Augustus had ordered a census to be taken throughout the empire (Luke 2:1–3). In

Rome itself all citizens were nominally enrolled in one of the tribes from which the city's population had originally been drawn. The tribes had long ceased to have any genetic significance. But they remained as the essential units lying at the base of Rome's constitution, on which the whole structure was built. They no longer lay within either ethnic or geographical boundaries. Members could be widely scattered, some tending farms and vineyards on the plains of Latium, others dwelling in the city itself. But to vote, a man had to be present in Rome, however far he had to travel. Today the word "tribute" reminds us that men were taxed tribe by tribe, while the word "tribune" recalls the days when high officers of state were appointed to safeguard the interests of the individual tribes before the Senate.

In Joseph's day this form of government, through tribal units, was still Rome's traditional style of administration, and she applied it, with necessary modifications, throughout her empire. So when the census was taken, every family had to register at the town with which their tribe was identified and which, in modern terms, would be called their tribal capital.

The census was announced after Joseph's betrothal, and the birth of Mary's child was very near. Nevertheless, there was no question of disobeying the order. The couple had perforce to leave Nazareth and go to Bethlehem, the registration centre for all those descended from the now almost legendary David. The journey was long and not without peril for Mary, so near to her time. But Rome's rules were strict, and not even a woman whose baby's birth was imminent could be exempted from the regulations. We can imagine

Joseph's solicitude for his young wife and his anxiety for her safety. We can imagine too how resentment against the stern Romans grew among the crowds who thronged the roads, making their weary way to their tribal capitals, leaving farms untended and crafts neglected. Mary was only one of many women in like condition forced to undergo the perils of a long journey. How harsh were the Romans and how tyrannous their rule! When would the true kingdom be renewed, and when would peace come again?

When Joseph and Mary arrived at Bethlehem, there was no room at the inn. This is significant. Since all the visitors at that time would have been members of the house of David, we catch a glimpse of the large number of men and women who could claim descent from the great king of long ago. Whenever dreams of the kingdom most abounded, these folk no doubt became the objects of speculation and expectation. So, because of the throng, Joseph could find no better place to lodge in than a stable for oxen.

But it was not only among the Jews that rumours of the expected birth of the true king were circulating. There were in Jerusalem at that time three Magi. The Magi were the hereditary priests of Persia, learned in their own religion and famous throughout the world for their skills in divining the future. There had long been a fellow feeling between the Persians and the Jews. The two nations had frequently been at war. In conflict they had learned to respect one another and had become familiar with one another's ways. Both worshipped one God and despised the pagan nations who worshipped many. Both recognised that the will of their God was opposed by the forces of evil led by God's adversary, who walked the earth, enticing men from truth and the law. The Jews called him Satan and the Persians knew him as Shaitan. With the Persians and Jews alike, priesthood was hereditary. The ancient religion of Persia was largely destroyed when the land was invaded by Islam in mediaeval days. But it was maintained by the Parsees—descendants of Persian refugees who, fleeing the swords of their conquerors, settled in India. Among them the old beliefs survive to this day.

Some 450 years before Joseph's day, Nehemiah, the cupbearer of Ataxerxes, the great king of Persia, was sent to Jerusalem as governor of Judea. Earlier conquerers had tried to destroy the culture and religion of the Jews. Not so Nehemiah. He restored many of the buildings of war-ravaged Jerusalem and rebuilt the city walls. The Persians treated the Jews, not as a vanquished and inferior nation, but as a people with whom they shared many ideals.

Against this background, it is probable that the three Magi who had "come from the East" were in Jerusalem as curious and scholarly visitors, seeking to learn something of the Jewish religion and perhaps to investigate the strange stories they had heard of a new kingdom. Matthew (2:2) tells us they asked where they could find the child who was born to be King of the Jews, "for we have seen his star in the East."

Later ages interpreted literally this mention of a star. The three wise men of legend cross the wide desert, with a great star hanging in the sky, beckoning them to Bethlehem. But was there indeed a physical star? If they came out of the East and if a physical star had guided them, then surely they would have seen the star in the West! Otherwise it would have led them out of Persia into the heart of Asia. There is another possible explanation. The Magi were famous for their powers of divination and their knowledge of astrology. Our words "magic" and "magician" bear testimony to this. They believed that the stars both governed and foretold the destinies of the world. The phrase that they had "seen his star" could therefore have meant that, in studying the heavens while they were yet in Persia, they had seen in their charts and calculations the star of a future prince in a neighbouring land. We have already seen how the dream of the coming Messiah had spread into the West. The same tales may have been heard in the sunlit towns and pillared temples of Persia. They would have provided a good starting point for astrologers to see grave portents in the stars foreshadowing the coming of a new king.

Meantime, in Bethlehem Mary gave birth to her child, Jesus. Everyone in the town knew that Joseph was of the house of David. The child had been born in the town of Micah's prophecy. Here at last was the promised king. The news spread rapidly throughout Bethlehem. We are told of shepherds who came to visit the baby made aware of the king's birth by a divine messenger. All the prophecies seemed now to have been fulfilled: the place of birth, Joseph's lineage, and the stories, perhaps already known to a few close friends, of a divine conception. Excitement mounted and the news quickly ran beyond Bethlehem. Confused rumours reached the ageing and unquiet King Herod, brooding in his palace and obsessed by the dangers that beset him.

Jealous as ever for the security of his throne, he summoned his priests and learned men, asking them what they knew about the birth of the Anointed One—the king who, if rumour were true, would displace him. They answered him by quoting Micah's prophecy: "But thou, Bethlehem Ephratah, though thou be little among the thousands of Judah, yet out of thee shall he come forth unto me that is to be ruler in Israel . . ." (Micah 5:2).

To the extent that Herod was a Jew, he gave credence to the ancestral legend and was terrified. For if the promised king were born, then he himself, who reigned with no more rights than Rome's armed support could bestow, would have to give place to the mysterious and semidivine claimant. But to the extent that Herod was a cosmopolitan and cynical man of the world, he needed more certain knowledge than quotations from the ancient Scriptures could yield. Were the rumours true? Had the child been born? Could the baby be identified and so perhaps destroyed?

He had heard of the presence in Jerusalem of the three Magi. Perhaps from these wise men, so skilled in divination, he could find the certainty he craved. Forthwith he sent to Jerusalem, summoned them to his presence, and despatched them to Bethlehem with orders to seek out the infant king and report back to him.

Whether or not they had been guided to Judea by an actual and physical star, they certainly needed no such star to lead them to Bethlehem, for King Herod himself ordered them thither. Moreover, when they arrived, they needed no mystical powers to identify the baby. All Bethlehem was agog with the story that at last the prophecy had been fulfilled. The three Magi were able to go straight to the stable where Joseph and Mary were lodged. They gave the child gifts of gold, frankincense, and myrrh. It is still the custom among the Parsees of India to place gold coins in the hands of newborn children, to bring them good luck and future prosperity. Fire is the central symbol of the Persian religion, symbolising the lambent purity of their God. To this day their descendants in India kindle a fire of sweet-scented sandalwood at all their ceremonies. On it they sprinkle incense, so that the perfumed smoke may be pleasing to the worshippers and to their God. So the Magi gave the child the usual present of gold, lit their sacred fire, and sprinkled on it the precious resins of frankincense and myrrh, as part of an accustomed ceremony of good fortune for newborn children. These three gifts were seen by later generations in the West, unfamiliar with Persian practice, as special offerings to a future king, both symbolising and recognising his regality. But more probably they were the usual gifts which any Persian priest would have offered to any child.

Having satisfied themselves that the infant Jesus fulfilled the conditions of the prophecy, compassion prompted them to defy Herod's instructions. They knew the bloody history of his reign. They had met him and knew him to be a man dedicated to the idea of power and sick with the fear of losing it. He had not hesitated to slaughter all who might challenge his kingship—Mariamne, his first wife, and his own sons. The dry comment of Augustus Caesar on hearing the news was that he would rather be Herod's pig than his son!

His throne and crown had been defended by a moat of blood. The Magi knew that once he could identify the child of the prophecy, he would not hesitate to add one more murder to the many which had marked his cruel reign. So, disobeying the old king's orders and not without peril to themselves, they did not return to his palace but went back to their own country.

When the three wise men failed to return, Herod was moved to great anger. The disappearance of the Magi seemed final proof that the prophesied king had been born; had they visited Bethlehem and found nothing, there would have been no reason for them to risk his wrath by fleeing to their own country. They could have returned to his court and told him, to his comfort, that no such child had been born.

His anxiety to safeguard the future of his throne and dynasty was savagely renewed, and he turned once more to murder. He ordered his soldiers to march to Bethlehem and there to slaughter all the boys who had been born there within the last two years. Nor was he content to order these murders in Bethlehem alone, but did so right down to the coast. He then slept securely, certain that this infant rival had been destroyed.

The slaughter of the innocents provides a significant commentary on the trial which Jesus was to undergo some thirty years later. For it offers clear evidence that King Herod, though he ruled as a puppet king under the suzerainty of Rome, retained the power of life and death over his subjects. Obsessed as he was with the safety of his royal state and knowing the invincibility of Rome, it is inconceivable that he would have committed this atrocity without sure knowledge that, within the then political framework, his action could not lawfully be challenged. There can be little doubt that his son, Herod II, before whom Jesus was to appear, possessed the same rights. Yet these rights were not exercised and Jesus was returned to the Roman authorities for final sentence.

Herod's savagery was in vain. Joseph (as the devout would say) was warned in a dream of Herod's intentions and of the mortal peril in which his son stood. Or (as others would say), knowing how rife were the rumours of the new king and aware of Herod's reputation, he realised the dangers which beset him. Accordingly, before Herod's troops entered Bethlehem to do their bloody work, he had secretly left the city with Mary and the child, had fled westwards, crossed the Sinai Desert, and had found safety in Egypt, far from the jurisdiction of King Herod.

The tale carries echoes of the events which had taken place in the time of Moses a thousand years before. As the Jewish people, fleeing from their bondage in Egypt, were divinely led through the Red Sea, crossing the perilous desert of Sinai to the land of Canaan, so Joseph and Mary, with their son, retraced that path out of Canaan back into Egypt. As God in his wrath had ordered the angel of death to ravage the land of Egypt, cutting down the firstborn, so had the children of Bethlehem perished. Stranger still: The firstborn of the Jewish people had been passed over by the angel of death. They had fulfilled the order of Moses, marking the doorposts of their houses with the sign of the blood of the sacrificial lamb so that death might recognise the homes in which they dwelt and so pass over them. The innocents who died on that dreadful day in Bethlehem, before the eyes of their shrieking mothers and anguished fathers, became, as it were, the sacrificial lambs by the sign of whose blood death passed over their infant king. And later he too was destined to play the part of the sacrificial lamb so that, as his followers believed, death might pass over the whole world. He was to die at the time of the Passover, the feast which commemorated the marking of the doorposts in Egypt a thousand years before with the blood of the lamb.

# 5

# Pontius Pilate

In 4 B.C. poor King Herod died as he had lived, sick with apprehension about the future of his kingdom, consumed by anxiety to perpetuate his dynasty, and yet reluctant to see his royal powers pass on to the next generation. As death drew near, he ordered the execution of his son Antipater. Only his increasing sickness prevented the sentence from being carried out. Five days later, after vainly attempting suicide, he died. His will revealed that he proposed to divide his kingdom between three of his sons. Herod Antipas was to become ruler of Galilee and Peraea; Archelaus, king of Judea; and Philip, ruler of those lands beyond Galilee which had been added to Herod's dominions by Augustus Caesar.

As we have seen in an earlier section, the Jewish

people feared that any prince from Herod's family would prove a bloody and tyrannous ruler. Augustus Caesar, to whom they sent a swift delegation, received them in the Temple of Apollo in order to discuss their petition. The speed with which they sent this delegation suggests that they had planned it even before old Herod died. Their resentment against him must have been bitter for them to be moved to seek government by an alien and pagan authority rather than by a Jewish king.

Simultaneously with the Jewish delegation Archelaus and his two brothers, Herod Antipas and Philip, also journeyed to Rome to plead with the emperor to implement King Herod's will. Augustus Caesar reached a compromise. He met the request of the Jews to the extent that he withheld from Archelaus the title of king. But he executed the main purpose of old Herod's will by giving to each of the princes the lands which their father had left them. None would have the title of king. Each took the title of tetrarch, that is, one of three rulers.

Perhaps Augustus was moved to seek a compromise by disturbing news which was then coming out of Palestine. A group of militant nationalists had risen in arms against the Roman power. The rebellion was put down only after Varus, the governor of Syria, had marched two legions southwards from Syria to assist the local garrison.

Ideas of rebellion and of throwing off the Roman yoke by force of arms had long smouldered in Jewish hearts. With Herod dead, they remembered with renewed passion the great days of their kingdom under David and Solomon. Resentment against their present ills fed the old dreams of restoring both the visible and invisible kingdoms.

A man named Judas, of Galilee, an extremist who believed in violence, seized the opportunity to foster rebellion. He laid no claim to be king, nor did he invoke the Messianic dream. But he was the avowed leader of the militant wing of the Jewish resistance movement.[1] He called his countrymen to arms, and thousands rallied to him.

He bore a name that was honourable in Jewry. It was Judas Maccabaeus who, generations earlier, had fought for and won the freedom of the nation; and to his family, the Maccabees, the kingdom had been given. They became the Hasmonean dynasty into which King Herod had married in a vain attempt to stabilise his position.

More recently another Judas had avenged the affront offered by Herod to the Jewish nation when, in defiance of the Second Commandment, the king had set up the great golden eagle in the Temple precincts. This Judas, with a companion called Mattahias, had destroyed the eagle, and both had been executed by Herod as martyrs to their faith. Now another Judas had arisen, and under his leadership perhaps the glory of the visible kingdom would revive, the ranks of Rome would be broken, the alien and tyrannical legate would be destroyed, and Judea would once more live in freedom under God and her own king.

Judas' gallant attempt to win back the kingdom by the sword failed, but not without heavy fighting. Although the troops which the governor of Syria led against him were mainly auxiliaries rather than regular Roman soldiers, they had been trained in war by Romans and were part of the empire's invincible war machine. They crushed the rebellion with skill and brutality. After it was put down, they crucified some two thousand of the rebels, an event which grimly reminds us that the Crucifixion was not a unique event. The Jewish people were made brutally familiar with the hideous crosses and the slow agonies of the dying men, which were the signs both of Rome's anger and of the savagery of her power. When, later, Jesus came to the choice with which he was faced in the Garden of Gethsemane, his decision was made with a full and vivid knowledge of the torments through which he had to pass and of the bitterness of the cup which was prepared for him.

In the face of these massive difficulties, Augustus Caesar had an important decision to make. To have denied the Jews their plea would have been to increase their resistance and to feed the flames of militant nationalism. But to cast out the princes of old Herod's family would have been to give up one of the most useful instruments of power which Rome possessed in the province.

So, as a result of this compromise, for the men of Judea, in spite of the plea submitted to Augustus by their delegates, the hated house of Herod continued in power. Their kingdom was now split into three fragments, and it seemed that the greatness of the kingdom had finally passed.

The new ruler, Archelaus, proved as tyrannous as Herod, and the people grew increasingly restive. If their ancient kingdom had become a mere playground for capricious and selfish kings, would it not be wiser to recognise that real power lay with Rome and to seek the more orderly government which direct rule from Caesar might provide?

Therefore in Josephus' words:

> In the tenth year of the ruler's government the principal Jews and Samaritans united in complaining of his tyrannical conduct to Augustus; who thereupon sent his agent from Rome to Archelaus, commanding him to repair . . . immediately into his presence. . . . On their arrival in the city, Augustus heard the charge and the defence. He sentenced Archelaus to banishment, sending him to Vienne in Gaul, and confiscated all his wealth.[2]

Thus in A.D. 6 the kingdom ended and Judea formally became a full Roman province. The emperor sent out Cyrenius, a senator and former consul, to govern Syria. Coponius, a senior cavalry commander, was sent at the same time as governor of Judea.

So the Jewish people had been granted their petition. Their proud and unwelcome king was gone, a wretched exile in Gaul; and the imperial government, known to be stern but expected to be just, now ruled over them. But any joy they felt was short-lived.

The first task of Coponius, the imperial legate, was to assess the territory for the levying of taxes, which were now payable to the Roman authorities and not to their own king. This involved a new census and the assessment of the wealth of every town, village, and farm. Roman officials and Jewish officers in the pay of Rome travelled through the resentful and sullen countryside. They counted the flocks, judged the fertility of the land, listed the crops, arrogantly intruding on the peaceful life of the inhabitants.

With Archelaus gone, Rome moved into the city of Jerusalem itself. The prefect of Judea had his military headquarters in Herod's great fortress named the Antonia in honour of his dead friend and patron, Mark Antony. There a cohort of troops was permanently stationed to police the city and the land around. As a symbol of Rome's sovereignty over all matters, both secular and spiritual, the prefect took over all those rights which had been the prerogative of King Herod. These included the safekeeping of the high priest's ritual vestments. These garments, sacred symbols of the Jewish religion, were now kept under lock and key in a barracks loud with the ringing footfalls and alien voices of pagan soldiers. The holy robes were released at the seasons of the great festivals, but only at the pleasure of the prefect. So the high priest came to be increasingly dependent on Rome's favour, holding office only while he retained the confidence of the prefect.

The prefect himself took up his official residence at Caesarea, where more troops were quartered. This was a Romanised town with public buildings after the Roman fashion and with a great theatre where contests and spectacles were displayed.

Despite the presence of foreign troops, the Temple authorities jealously maintained their right to maintain their own armed police force—the Temple Guards. These kept law and order in the Temple area and were the secular arm of the Sanhedrin—the Jewish religious council.

Far away in Rome, the ageing Augustus safeguarded

his personal power by ensuring that local governors were frequently changed. Later ages vindicated this policy, for when it was discontinued, army governors, spending many years in their own provinces and secure in the accustomed loyalty of their troops, declared themselves emperors, so that the great monolith of the Roman state was shattered and finally fell.

So Augustus allowed Coponius a bare three years of office, as he did for the two men who succeeded him. Then in A.D. 14 Augustus Caesar died and the new emperor, Tiberius, followed a different policy. He preferred his provincial governors and prefects to remain in office for many years, on the basis of "better the devil you know than the devil you don't know."

During the first year of his reign he appointed Valerius Gratus as governor of Judea, who held the post uninterruptedly for eleven years. Gratus took an active interest in the Jewish priesthood and made it very clear that the appointment of high priest lay in his gift. During the eleven years of his governorship he removed no fewer than four high priests, appointing men of his own choice in their place. Cynics might suggest that his main motive was greed, since at every change of high priest he could demand bribes from the contending candidates! His last appointment, made in A.D. 18, was a man named Caiaphas, the son-in-law of Annas, who had been high priest when Gratus first arrived in Judea. Whether Caiaphas possessed the qualities of justice and erudition appropriate to his office is doubtful, as further events will show. He had some claim to the position as Annas' son-in-law, but he clearly owed his office entirely to Roman patronage. He was well aware of this, having seen his predecessors come and go, appointed and deposed at the whim of the Roman prefect. He knew himself to be totally dependent upon the goodwill of the Roman authorities, and as we shall see from his attitude and actions at Jesus' trial, this caused him to be politically rather than spiritually motivated.

In A.D. 26 Valerius Gratus departed from Judea, leaving the Roman authority firmly established in the province. Although Herod and his brothers were rulers of Judea, although the Jewish council (the Sanhedrin) deliberated on the nation's religious affairs, and although a high priest performed the ancient rites within the Temple, the stark realities of power lay in the fortress of the Antonia with the cohort of Roman troops and in the prefect's palace in Caesarea. The Jewish authorities still issued their traditional coinage, with which the people paid their annual tax for the maintenance of the Temple. But side by side with it and more abundant in shop and marketplace was the coinage of Rome—of bronze, silver, and gold. The older coinage bore the image of Augustus Caesar and the newer pieces that of Tiberius. With this Roman coinage the people paid their taxes to the prefect's officers for the upkeep of the troops who oppressed them and of the stern officers and officials who so completely ordered their lives.

Such was the situation when the new prefect, Pontius Pilate, arrived in Judea in A.D. 26. This was the man who, a few years later, was to order the crucifixion of Jesus, despite having found him guiltless of the charges laid against him, yielding to the clamour of the mob rather than to the dictates of his conscience.

He is remembered as the procurator of Judea. In fact, it is very doubtful whether he held that office. In the more important provinces the Roman authorities normally appointed two senior officials. The seniormost was the proconsul. This was a man who had held in Rome the supreme office of consul, which, even after the establishment of the empire by Augustus, continued to be held in the highest esteem. After a consul had completed his year in office, he retained, as a proconsul, the consular power of life and death which consuls possessed, but which he could now exercise only in the provinces. It was thus administratively convenient to appoint proconsuls as governors of the provinces, since with this power they could fully represent the authority of the Senate.

There were some dangers in this system, since a proconsul's authority was, within his province, equal to that of the emperor's. Augustus therefore took two steps to curb the power of the proconsuls. First, he kept the governorship of some of the more important provinces in his own gift. Second, in each proconsular province he personally appointed a second officer to keep a wary eye on the governor. This was the procurator, ostensibly appointed to deal with taxes and to supervise the civil administration of the province; he was in fact the personal representative of the emperor. His task was to ensure that the proconsul did not overstep his own authority or become a threat to the central government.

Thus it was that proconsular provinces had two officers—a governor and a procurator. But Judea was not such a province. It came under the authority of the governor of Syria, and the highest officer within Judea itself held the title of prefect. This was the designation of all Pilate's predecessors. That he himself bore it is borne out by an inscribed stone discovered in the theatre at Caesarea in 1961.[3] In the inscription Pontius Pilate is mentioned by name as *Praefectus Iudaeae.* Clearly, by the time the Gospels came to be written in the form that we know them, the finer details of the administration in Judea had been forgotten.

Much is known about Pilate's career. Josephus gives a full account of his term of office in Judea, and there is another source, the writer Philo. The facts they recount help to explain Pilate's vacillating behaviour during the trial of Jesus. Before that trial he had more than once been confronted by the sullen and unshakeable obstinacy of the Jewish people whenever their religious principles were threatened. Although they were a conquered and subject people and although he possessed supreme authority over them and had troops at his disposal, he had twice been forced to yield to their massive demonstrations of protest. Fear of open rebellion and of the damage that such rebellion would inflict on his public career had on each occasion forced him to give way to their clamour.

According to Philo, Pilate once decided to set up a number of votive shields in the younger Herod's palace in Jerusalem.[4] These shields, plated with pure gold, represented the military power of Rome and would remind both Herod and his people that the royal authority depended ultimately on the force of Roman arms, symbolised by the golden shields. But the Jewish people saw his action as an insult to their holy city, to their ruler, and to the honour and glory of their ancient faith. Neither the stern figures of the Roman troops patrolling the city nor the knowledge of their own defencelessness deterred the people from voicing their discontent.

A delegation called upon Pilate, led by four princes, all sons of Herod the Great. Pilate was not to be persuaded. Sternly he told them that the golden shields would remain in the palace and that he would not and could not retract his orders. The Jews decided, as was their right, to appeal directly to Caesar. Tiberius, to maintain peace in the province, ordered Pilate to remove the shields and to place them in the temple dedicated to Augustus in the city of Caesarea. From this event, each side drew its own lesson. Pilate learned that he dared not in future ride roughshod over the Jews' religious sensitivities, since the central government in Rome would never support him in such a course. And the Jews learned that, stern and unbending though Pilate might appear, they ultimately held the upper hand and could, by public protest and by the merest hint of disorder, force the prefect to yield to their wishes.

In the case of the second episode, they had no need to appeal to Caesar. Josephus tells us that it was the custom for some of the troops normally stationed at Caesarea to spend the winter in Jerusalem.[5] On this occasion Pilate ordered them to bring their standards with them and to set them up in the city. Some of these standards bore a bronze bust of the emperor and therefore constituted a breach of Jewish law. The Second Commandment expressly forbad the use of such emblems and devices. No former governor had ever before defied the people's wishes by bringing such graven images into the city. What added to Pilate's offence was that the standards were brought to Jerusalem at dead of night and furtively set up unknown to the inhabitants. When in the morning the people saw what had been done, they assembled in great numbers and went to Pilate in Caesarea requesting that these obnoxious images be removed. Pilate refused, and although they remained in Caesarea for several days, he was obdurate in his refusal, claiming that to comply with their request would be a personal insult to the emperor.

After a week's fruitless discussion Pilate ordered out a patrol of fully armed soldiers. With them as escort, he went to the great open-air theatre, followed by a throng of Jews, all clamouring for a favourable answer to their request. In the theatre Pilate mounted a dais which had been prepared and ordered all the Jews who had followed him to leave. Those that did not, he declared, would be slaughtered on the spot by the soldiers. There was a vast concourse of people, for the delegation from Jerusalem had been joined by large numbers from Caesarea. None made any move to leave the theatre. Indeed, on hearing Pilate give the order to his troops, they flung themselves to the ground, stretching out their necks in readiness to receive the soldiers' swords.

Pilate was confronted by the choice of a savage and scandalous massacre or a withdrawal of his instructions. He chose the latter. As in the case of the golden shields, he had to back down. The offending portraits of Caesar were removed from the city of Jerusalem, and Pontius for the second time had avoided a head-on collision with Jewish religious opinion. But he had done so at the cost of yielding to the stubbornness of the crowd.

His surrender was all the more remarkable in the light of the almost religious devotion paid by the Romans to their legionary standards. They were the symbol of a legion's soul, and men would die rather than allow them to be captured or see them retreat.

There was yet another affair in which Pilate had to face the anger of the Jewish people. During his prefecture he decided to have an aqueduct built to bring water into Jerusalem. Since the improved water supply would benefit the people generally and the Temple in particular, he asked for a contribution to be made from Jewish funds. He was refused, and again there was a confrontation. This time Pilate ordered out a patrol of soldiers in plain clothes. They carried no swords but had been issued with riot weapons—staffs and bludgeons—which they hid under their cloaks. They surrounded the rioting crowds, who were vociferously protesting against Pilate. He gave the order and the riot squad of soldiers moved in, savagely beating the crowd with their clubs and staffs so that many died. Again he was taught the lesson that to resist the mob was to bring about violent and tragic consequences.

Such was the man in whose hands the mortal destiny

of Jesus was to lie. In him severity and appeasement alternated. He could go so far in fulfilling his duty but would retreat in the face of popular clamour. And it was in this way that he acted, moved by expediency rather than by any sense of justice, at the tragic trial of Jesus.

# 6

# The Baptism by Water

Pilate had not long been in office when he heard news of a strange Jewish preacher who had gone into the wilderness—the uncultivated lands in the north, by the River Jordan. John, for that was the name of this holy man, was summoning all to come to him, to be cleansed of their sins in the waters of that river. Multitudes flocked to hear him and to receive at his hands the ritual cleansing which washed away their past sins. He warned his listeners that the day of God's judgement would soon be on them. He claimed to be no more than the herald of that judgement and the forerunner of a mysterious and powerful person whom he did not name but who would follow him.

The idea that washing in water freed men from past sins was neither new nor unique. Ovid, who was writing during the reign of Augustus, refers to this practice. True, he sees it as a comfortable superstition rather than as a valid rite. For he exclaims that a man is far too easygoing if he believes that the waters of a river can wash away the woeful crime of slaughter. But his words are good evidence for belief in the rite among some pagan Romans.[1] The Hindus, from time immemorial, have washed away their sins by bathing in the holy waters of the Ganges River. The Jews themselves had always believed in the purifying value of a ritual washing. All converts to the faith had not only to be circumcised but to have the sins of their former life washed away with water.

What was new in John's call to baptism was that he was neither seeking proselytes to the Jewish religion nor limiting his mission to members of that faith. He was calling on men who were already Jews to undergo the rite which had hitherto been reserved for converts. He was implying that they had lapsed into sin as grievous as that of any pagan; and just as a pagan, on embracing the Jewish faith, had to have his sins washed away, so they must undergo the same rite and turn away from sin before meeting the forthcoming day of judgement.

Hitherto we have spoken of the Jewish religion as a single and uniform faith. In fact it was divided into several sects, which Josephus describes.[2]

First were the Pharisees, simple and austere, with the firm belief that the righteous would enjoy happiness and that the wicked would be condemned to torments, chains, and darkness. In their creed there was great devotion but little compassion. Josephus independently confirms what the New Testament tells us, that the

Pharisees tended to be self-righteous and believed themselves to be better than other men.

Second were the Sadducees, who rejected the idea of an afterlife and who held that man's only obligation was to observe the law on earth. This he had to do out of pure and unselfish devotion, there being neither reward nor punishment after the extinction of death.

Third were the Essenes, who accepted the immortality of the soul and who held that justice was the chief of all virtues. While paying the temple dues, they did not attend the official rites in the Temple. They held all things in common and lived as farmers in close communities. They were strict in their morals and rigid in their conversation.

Fourth was the sect which Judas of Galilee founded during the uprising already described. They had beliefs similar to those of the Pharisees. But in addition they held freedom and liberty in the highest esteem and would accept no superior other than God. They would call, therefore, no man master, since for them the idea that any man could dominate another was totally unacceptable. That they should have an alien and pagan authority set over them was very anathema. They represented the militant wing of the Jewish people who were prepared to overthrow Roman rule by force of arms and who many times made gallant but vain attempts to do so. Josephus gave them the name of Zealots. They had many sympathisers who were not formal members of the sect but who wholeheartedly shared their militant patriotism and their hatred for all things Roman.

The discovery of the Dead Sea Scrolls has shone a

great light on the beliefs and practices of a community of men living at Qumran. These, like the Essenes, with whom they had much in common, lived an austere communal life. They followed the law with the devotion of the Sadducees and outdid the Pharisees in their search for righteousness. It has been suggested that John was from that community. If so, one of their practices is worthy of mention. In their search for godliness and in their eagerness never to remain in a state of sin, each day they ritualistically washed away their wrongdoings in water, in a kind of daily baptism.

Ideas of this kind may well have prompted John in his belief that baptism of converts was not enough but that even devoted followers of the law should undergo the ritual if they were to come anew to the worship of the true God, cleansed of all sin.

The word "baptism" is Greek in origin and is derived from a verb meaning to dip and, by extension, to dye. As cloth was cleansed and dyed with the bright hues that men wished to wear, so were men to be dipped into the purifying waters and to be given the colour of sanctity and the bright hue of holiness.

Thirty years earlier, as we have seen, rumours of the king, of the Anointed One, were rife, and hopes ran high that he would soon appear, to liberate his people from spiritual sin and earthly oppression, restoring both the invisible and the visible kingdoms. These hopes did not die with the flight of Joseph and Mary into Egypt. Indeed, John's story provides clear evidence of its survival, for when John was baptising in the River Jordan, priests went out from Jerusalem, whither the news of his activities had spread, and asked him whether he was indeed the Anointed One (John 1:20). When he answered, "I am not the Christ" (the Anointed One), they asked whether he was Elias come again. The priests, who were Pharisees, then challenged him, seeking to know by what right he was giving baptism "if thou be not that Christ nor Elias" (John 1:25).

Essentially John's purpose was not merely to call the virtuous to renew their virtue but those who had sinned, in order that they might be led back to God through the path of repentance. Luke (3:12 and 13) records the startling fact that he even baptised publicans.

To the Jewish people, as to provincials throughout the empire, the *publicani* had become symbols of all that was oppressive and evil. They were the collectors of the taxes which Rome imposed upon the conquered people. They were not themselves direct representatives of the central government, for Rome early realised that to set up a tax-collecting organisation throughout her vast empire would be immensely costly. So she devised a system which, though elegant in its conception, made the provincials the victims of cruel extortion.

Once the authorities had assessed the total amount of tax due from any province, the actual collection was handed over to private enterprise. The matter was put to public tender, and joint stock companies would submit bids, stating what percentage of the official tax they would pay net to the central government and how little they would keep to cover their own expenses. The government would accept the highest tender, that is to say, the bid which contained the lowest amount for expenses. The groups of men who put in these offers were usually the Knights of Rome, the wealthy middle class. Having pared down their expenses on paper, the only possible way in which they could make a profit was by extortion and by claiming far more from the taxpayers than the official money tax. When it came to taxes in kind, they would use oversize measures for the corn and wine and olives which they collected. The true measure went to the authorities, and the excess went into their pockets.

The *publicani* were the agents of these infamous tax-collecting companies and personally received all the odium which their companies' malpractices merited. They became a byword for dishonesty, tyranny, and unscrupulousness. When, as not infrequently occurred, they were themselves natives of the province, then they became symbols of the additional sins of treachery and treason.

That John should have baptised even publicans was therefore considered worthy of special mention, for such would normally be rejected by holy men in pursuit of righteousness and justice. But John was calling sinners to repentance, and when the publicans, having been baptised, asked him what they should do, he did not bid them give up their odious calling. He simply told them to exact no more than that which had been appointed to them (Luke 3:13). We must remember the evil reputation of the publicans when we come to learn of Jesus conversing with them and how this must have outraged his more self-righteous contemporaries.

John was also approached by others representing the unwelcome power of the state, for we are told that "the soldiers on guard asked him, "What of us, What are we to do?'" (Luke 3:14). John had established himself on one of the main trade routes so that, as Monsignor Knox points out, these soldiers may well have been those on guard at the customshouses. John did not spurn them as the violent and pagan oppressors of his nation. He was content to tell them not to use unnecessary violence, not to lay false information against anyone, and to be satisfied with their pay. Again we are reminded forcibly of Jesus, one of whose cures was effected at the request of no less a personage than a Roman centurion, the grim and armoured symbol of the hated foreign power.

John was always insistent that he was merely the precursor not only of the coming judgement but of a far greater one than himself whom, for all his own holy works, he was unworthy to serve even in the most menial tasks. In the East shoes are the ultimate symbol of uncleanness. They carry overtones of meaning that are absent to the Western ear. They must be put off not only when entering a holy place but when entering the home of a friend. To beat a man is an insult. To beat him with a shoe, a degradation. Thus, when John expressed his subordination to the towering greatness of the coming one by saying that he was not fit even to tie up the latter's shoes, he was using an expression of humility that would have come home most vividly to his listeners.

To him there now came his cousin Jesus, now some thirty years old, and requested John to baptise him.

If John had been a member of the Qumran community, as has been suggested, he would have followed their belief that there were to be two Messiahs. This was because that community saw the Messiah as fulfilling two functions, of kingship and of religious leadership. Properly to carry out the duties of a king the Messiah would have to be a descendant of the house of David, as foreshadowed in the prophecy of Isaiah. But as religious leader he would have to be a descendant of Levi, since only Levites could become priests. If John held this belief, he could well have found both figures merging in the person of Jesus. He knew that Jesus was of the house of David, since this was common knowledge. He himself was a Levite, and his mother was kin to Mary, the mother of Jesus. Although priesthood did not and does not descend in the female line, this might have provided sufficient link for John to accept Jesus as the long-awaited Messiah, uniquely able by birth and destiny to fulfil both the functions—temporal and spiritual—of that figure.

As we shall see, John probably knew Jesus already and was aware of his ideals and ambitions. Certainly he instantly recognised him as the one for whom he himself had acted merely as the harbinger. And he put to Jesus a question which for many still calls for an answer. If Jesus was indeed both the Son of God and God himself in human form, then he did not share in the curse of Adam or partake in the original sin with the burden of which every man was born. Nor, during his years on earth, could he have been guilty of any sin. It followed therefore that for him to undergo baptism was totally unnecessary. Even if that proposition could be answered, how could John presume to submit God himself to the rites of baptism?

Both questions are susceptible of the answer that Jesus, now just beginning his public mission, wished to set an example to the Jewish people and to demonstrate personally the universal need for the ritual of baptismal cleansing and for that inner repentance which was its very essence. But John's recorded words suggest that he himself found no satisfaction in such answers. For "John forbad him, saying 'I have need to be baptised of thee, and comest thou to me?' And Jesus answering said unto him 'Suffer it to be so now.'" Significantly Jesus added an explanation: "for thus it becometh us to fulfil all righteousness" (Matthew 2:14 and 15).

Jesus' baptism by John was the first recorded occasion on which the claim that he was the Son of God was advanced and, as it were, confirmed. For the evangelists are unanimous that the spirit of God, in the form of a dove, was seen to descend on Jesus and that a voice declared him to be the Son of God. In the Gospel according to St. John, St. John the Baptist himself made the declaration "and I saw and bare record that this is the Son of God" (John 1:34).

To a contemporary world the statements that the Holy Spirit appeared as a dove would have caused neither surprise nor bewilderment. Birds played an important part in religious observances. There was in the Roman world a special priesthood trained to interpret the flight of birds. These priests were known as augurs, and no one embarked on any important action without consulting them. Moreover, a man's soul was often said to have been seen ascending to heaven in the form of a bird soaring from the funeral pyre. One of the arguments brought forward in the Senate in support of the proposal to accept a dead emperor as a god was evidence that men had seen a great eagle rising from his bier and winging its way into the invisible heavens towards the homes of the immortal gods. It was accepted that Jove could reveal his purposes through the flight of birds and, by the same means, mark out a man for greatness.

So Jesus insisted on and accepted baptism at John's hands. And it was this baptism that marked the opening of his own ministry. He accepted the rite as possessing some special significance and immediately thereafter began to gather together disciples of his own. Had John been content to limit his preaching to the calling of sinners to repentance, to announcing the coming of a spiritual leader far greater than himself, and to public recognition of Jesus as that man, then it is highly unlikely that he would have caused Pilate more than a passing annoyance. He would have been irritated—little more—that once again his troublesome province was in the grip of some kind of religious hysteria. But John began to concern himself with matters which in Roman eyes were purely political and in which he had no right to meddle.

Herod, the son of Herod the Great and installed by the Romans as tetrarch of Galilee and Peraea, had married Herodias, his dead brother Philip's widow. Such a marriage was not permitted under Jewish law unless the dead brother had left no children. Then not only was it permitted to marry his widow, it was obligatory to do so, so that one might lie with the widow in one's brother's place, beget children with her, and by substitution ensure that his seed would not perish from the earth. The story of Ruth is evidence of this practice, for on her husband's death, she married his kinsman, Boaz.

But in the case of Herod and Herodias, this condition had not been fulfilled. Herodias had already borne a daughter, Salome, to Philip. So Herod's marriage was against the holy law. However, no one dared to rebuke a ruler. Caiaphas, the high priest, who, like Herod, knew that his continuance in office depended on the favour of the Romans, certainly had no desire to meddle.

Nor indeed had Pontius Pilate, the prefect. Although there was no love lost between him and Herod (Luke 23:12), the problem was one that concerned Jewish law alone. The Romans themselves had no very rigid ideas about incest or about the permitted degrees of kinship in marriage. A few years later Emperor Claudius was to marry his own niece. Nero was to marry his own sisters—though certainly this was felt to be something of a scandal. It was no concern of Pilate's if Herod wished to contract a marriage sinful in the eyes of his own bigoted people but perfectly acceptable to any civilised Roman. His anxiety not to become involved in matters concerning the Jewish religion (as evidenced by the stories of the shields and the standards) made him even more detached about the whole situation.

But John had no such scruples. He who had publicly told one of the hated publicans how to behave in future—he who had addressed soldiers of the army of occupation in peremptory tones of instruction was not afraid to criticise the tetrarch. He began publicly to rebuke Herod for the sin of his marriage. Herod's reaction was as savage as his father's might have been.

Matthew (14:3–11) gives a full account of how he had John thrown into prison and later beheaded at the request of Herodias' daughter. Josephus confirms John's death at Herod's hand but with different details.[3] He explains that the marriage was doubly sinful, for Herodias was not only the widow of Herod's brother Philip, she was also his niece, being the daughter of their brother Aristobulus. Furthermore, to marry her he had to put away his first wife, an event which led him into war with her outraged supporters. Herod's army was overwhelmed and he was compelled to seek the support of the governor of Syria, thus still further increasing his humiliating dependence on Rome.

Josephus also confirms the biblical description of John the Baptist:

> His custom was to exhort the Jews to the love and practice of every virtue; recommending them to regulate their lives by the rules of piety and justice; urging the necessity of regeneration by baptism and a new life; and insisting that it was not by abstaining from any particular vice, but by a constant and uniform course of goodness, that the benefit of such regeneration was to be acquired. By the holiness of his life, the Baptist had acquired great reputation and influence among the people; and his disciples were extremely numerous.

Josephus does not record John's public rebuke as Herod's motive for killing him. He explains that Herod, realising John's growing authority and knowing the immense number of his followers, feared that he might raise up a popular uprising against him. The combination of religious eminence and a multitude of supporters was a perilous matter. And he who stood at the head was best destroyed. So Herod sent him as a prisoner to Macarus with orders that he should be put to death, and the bloody deed was done—a deed that was both a portent and a precedent.

However John's death befell, news of it would have come to Pilate. He might have dismissed it with a shrug. Herod had the right to do what he would with his own. But once more Pilate was made aware of the degree of unrest and violence which could so easily trouble his province, because of the absurd religious sensitivities of his stubborn people and of the ridiculous enthusiasm with which they followed after new prophets. How lacking they were in the classical virtue of moderation and how viciously immoderate even in their virtues!

Herod's fear of John the Baptist did not die with the murdered man. He remained a haunted soul, as the records show, for by now Jesus had begun to teach the people, and news of this came to Herod's ears. The reports showed that the teachings of Jesus closely echoed those of John. Poor ghost-ridden Herod was certain that the new teacher was the dead John, risen horribly from the grave to renew his rebukes. And he said to those about him: "This is John the Baptist; he is risen from the dead; and therefore mighty works do show forth themselves in him" (Matthew 14:2). As John had been asked whether he was Elias come again, so Jesus was at first taken for John the Baptist revisiting the earth from the grave.

Did a memory of those fears return yet again to Herod when later Jesus was brought before him for judgement? Was this the old nightmare come again? Was there to be no end to this confrontation with strange and holy men? Was he destined, like his father, to be perpetually doomed to defend his authority through the blood and on the bodies of other men?

# 7

# The Lost Dream

We have seen how John the Baptist was asked by the priests whether he was the Anointed One—the Messiah. Here is direct evidence of the dream of the kingdom's restoration and of the great one who was to be born to rule it.

Mysteriously, this is the first such evidence since the events in Bethlehem some thirty years earlier. When Joseph and Mary went to David's city to be entered in the census, the dream of the kingdom and of the coming ruler was obviously very much in men's minds. Moreover, after Jesus had been born, many were certain that the prophecies had been fulfilled and that the king had come.

Old Herod had been sure—sure enough to order the savage murder of all the baby boys in the neighbourhood. The shepherds had been sure; they had in a vision seen God's messenger announcing the new king's birth and had gone unerringly to do him homage. The three Magi had been sure and, to save the infant king, defied Herod and fled silently away.

Then—until the priests' question to John—total silence. What had happened to that ancient and seemingly immortal dream during those thirty years?

Once the Christian faith had been established, the birth at Bethlehem came to be seen as the entering of a monarch into the capital of his kingdom. With the Roman emperors there grew up a traditional ceremony involving such a formal entry. After the death of Nero, when the direct and collateral lines of Julius and Augustus were alike extinct, emperors were frequently appointed from among provincial commanders. Some never visited Rome, but for those who did so the event was one of immense symbolic importance, surrounded by imperial pomp and religious ritual. The occasion was known as the *Adventus Augusti*—the Coming of the Emperor. Special coins were struck to commemorate the event. These would depict the emperor, fully armed and mounted on a war charger, and usually bore the slogan *Adventus.*

To Christians in Rome after the time of Nero the birth at Bethlehem came to be seen as the coming of the world's king into his mortal kingdom, and to this day the occasion is celebrated under the name of Advent. True, this was a later development. But something of this magic and majesty was felt at the time of the birth itself. The shepherds must have shared their certainty with others. The citizens of Bethlehem must have discussed the portents and the mystery. Nor can it be believed that Herod's troops were unaware of the reason for their royal master's savage order and the hideous duty they had so cold-bloodedly to discharge. Certainly, too, news of the king's birth had spread abroad from the streets of Bethlehem, from Herod's towered court, and from the walled city of Jerusalem, where the three wise men must have shared their knowledge with many.

And yet, mysteriously, for thirty years the vision faded and the dream was lost. It vanished until the question was put to John the Baptist—was he the Anointed One?

Was the dream lost through certainty or doubt, through knowledge of hope fulfilled or in the bitterness of despair? Those who knew of the events in Bethlehem, certain that their promised king had been born, would have maintained a patient and loyal silence. Sure that the divine promise would be fulfilled, they were content to wait until the new leader of Israel was ready to announce himself. Others, having seen the failure of Zealot risings and religious revivals, had seen the swaggering power of Rome insolently increase. Such would have lapsed gradually into the listlessness of hope denied.

Thirty years was a long time to await the coming of the Anointed One since the rumours and certainties of the almost forgotten census. Among the Romans a boy came of age and put on the broad bordered toga of manhood when he was about fifteen; among the Jews boys came of age at thirteen. So twenty years after the birth of Jesus certainty might have begun to give way to doubt, and doubt to despair.

More mysterious than the loss of the dream was the loss of the man himself. Matthew (2:13–15) tells us how Joseph took Mary and the child from Bethlehem into Egypt to escape from Herod and that they stayed there until Herod's death. Matthew tells us that Joseph learned of Herod's death in a dream, in which an angel appeared to him. But he could have heard the news without divine intervention. We have already seen how, on Herod's death, his son Archelaus travelled to Rome to secure his inheritance at the hands of Augustus and how a delegation of Jews also went to the imperial city, requesting Augustus to set aside Herod's will and to appoint a Roman governor over them. News of Herod's death and of the political turmoil which it prompted would have swiftly spread throughout the Roman province of Egypt and unquestionably would have reached Joseph.

Indeed, it seems certain that Joseph had heard not only of Herod's death but of the moves (in the event unsuccessful) made by the Jewish people to prevent Archelaus from inheriting. For Matthew records that Joseph did not realise that Archelaus would be the ruler of Judea until after he had returned to his own country. Like that section of the Jewish people represented by the delegation, he feared that Archelaus would prove as tyrannous, oppressive, and cruel as his father. He did not again wish to place his child in jeopardy, and Matthew (2:22) tells us: "But when he heard that Archelaus did reign in Judaea in the room of his father

Herod, he was afraid to go thither; notwithstanding, being warned of God in a dream, he turned aside into the parts of Galilee."

From Matthew's narrative it is clear that Joseph left Egypt immediately after he heard of Herod's death but before he heard of Archelaus' accession to power. Herod died only a few months after the slaughter at Bethlehem. Therefore Joseph and his family were in Egypt for a matter of months at most. There is thus no mystery as to the whereabouts of Jesus between his infancy and boyhood. He was back in Nazareth.

The record itself is blank until Jesus was twelve, when Luke (2:42–49) tells us of his spending three days in the Temple at Jerusalem, listening to the teaching of learned men and putting his questions to them. Thenceforward there is a further silence of eighteen years until his baptism at the hands of John. Many attempts have been made to explain away these "lost years" of Jesus. There are legends as far afield as India, that he spent part of those eighteen years there learning something of the wisdom and philosophies of the East. There are legends too that he came to Britain as a young man with Joseph of Arimathea, who is said to have traded in tin from Cornwall to the Near East. It is an engaging legend without any firm evidence to substantiate it. It is best commemorated in William Blake's hymn:

> And did those feet in ancient time
> Walk upon England's mountains green?
> And was the holy Lamb of God
> On England's pleasant pastures seen?

And did the Countenance Divine
Shine forth upon our clouded hills?

The facts lie in obscurity, and nothing that is known can shine any light upon them. Blake cast his lines into the form of questions and not of assertions. However closely we study the material, no answers are to be found. Jesus may indeed have spent his time outside Judea, travelling southwards along Rome's organised trade routes to India or northwards to the remote island of Britain. But there is not a shred of firm evidence that he ever left Nazareth. The legends are engaging but contribute nothing to the truth.

What happened is no doubt as simple as the Gospel narrative. He grew up quietly in Nazareth, learning his father's trade, seeing the daily life of the people, and soaking himself in the Scriptures. When he came to die, he was known and described as a man from Nazareth. When he taught, his words were made vivid by the pastoral life of his fellow countrymen. His metaphors, like those of his forebear David in the Psalms, were drawn from the farms, pastures, hills, and olive groves of his native land. They are not the words of one who had been to strange places and studied alien religions under the palms of India or the oak and ash of Cornwall. He was a man not only of his own time but of his own land, and it is as such that he can best be understood.

Nor is there any mystery in Luke's story of his lingering in the Temple when he was twelve years old (Luke 2:42–49). This is not the sudden reappearance of a figure who had mysteriously vanished. It was Jesus' first important step towards spiritual maturity. All Jewish boys when they are thirteen (that is to say, upon completion of their twelfth year) are admitted as members of the synagogue. This is the Bar Mitzvah and this is no doubt the occasion which Luke is recording.

Then once more silence descends, and we hear no more of Jesus until his baptism at John's hands.

During these long years of waiting Joseph and Mary could not shed the dangerous burden of their knowledge. But they could do everything possible to keep it a secret within their own household. If their son was to fulfil his royal and spiritual role, then it was not for them to make any disclosure. It was for Jesus himself, when he had grown to maturity and was himself ready to embark on his perilous adventures, to announce his purpose in his own way. So they would have kept all that they knew as a closely guarded secret, shared proudly with one another and at most with such close relatives as they could trust. Among these would almost certainly have been John the Baptist. He was close kin to Jesus, since his mother, Elizabeth, was Mary's cousin (Luke 1:36). The two women had always been very close to each other. Years before, as soon as Mary knew that she was with child and had learned of her unborn child's origins and destiny, she went to Elizabeth's house. She found that Elizabeth, too, was pregnant. She revealed to Elizabeth all that she knew about her child, and the words ascribed to her by Luke—"My soul doth magnify the Lord"—were addressed to Elizabeth.

Mary stayed with her cousin for three months and did not leave until Elizabeth was about to give birth to her own son, whom she named John.

Luke's account thus confirms that Elizabeth was privy to the secret, which Mary had shared with her before the birth of Jesus. It is inconceivable that Mary did not, on her return from Egypt, similarly entrust Elizabeth with the knowledge of all that had taken place in Bethlehem—of the warning given to her by the Magi and of the recognition of Jesus by the shepherds.

Elizabeth's husband, Zaccharias, was also aware of the facts, for after John had been named, Zaccharias (who had earlier lost the use of speech) recovered his voice and spoke of the coming to Israel of "a horn of salvation for us in the house of his servant David."

John was three months older than Jesus. When we recall how close their mothers were to each other, it is reasonable to believe that they spent considerable time together, both as boys and as young men. When John, as a young man, showed signs of some special religious mission, it can be assumed that he too would have been admitted to the secret shared by the two families.

He would have had powerful reasons for maintaining the strictest secrecy. He would have been enjoined so to do by his parents, and strict obedience to one's parents' command was and is an essential component of the Jewish way of life. But there were more compelling reasons: Jesus was his kinsman—in the East such would be accounted brothers; and John knew the hideous dangers that would arise should the perilous truth of his royal birth and Messianic destiny be spread abroad.

Others who shared the secret would have had less

personal but equally strong reasons for maintaining silence. If they believed (and only such as did so knew that the prophecies had been fulfilled) that the Anointed One had been born, then they would have guarded the secret with religious zeal. No word of theirs would be allowed to bring back to the young man the bloody perils which had beset him in Bethlehem. The mystery of the lost dream becomes less mysterious when we see it as a tale suppressed rather than a tale forgotten.

Given that John was aware of the secret, then many of the details of his story become easier to understand. When he and Jesus were about thirty, it appears that each had decided that his time had come. It is difficult to believe that such close kinsmen did so without often consulting together and discussing their plans. Had they done so, then John's foretelling of a greater one than himself was the result of sure and certain knowledge. Knowing the secret both of Jesus' birth and intentions, he could not but see his own mission save as a prelude to that of his greater kinsman. Discussions between the two young men would also explain the similarities between their teachings. John called sinners to repentance; Jesus said, "There is more joy in heaven over one sinner who repenteth than over ninety-nine just men" (Luke 15:7). It was John who proclaimed the coming judgement; it was Jesus who in parable after parable described that judgement—the winnowing of the wheat from the chaff and the separation of the sheep from the goats.

The moment Jesus appeared among the crowd which surrounded John, the latter of course knew and recognised him. Before Jesus had approached him closely, he told the crowd that the great one who was to follow him was already in their midst. Perhaps he had not known that Jesus intended seeking baptism at his hands. The idea would have been unthinkable in the light of all that he knew of his kinsman, destined from the moment of his birth to become the Anointed One—a far greater man than himself. Hence John's sudden and almost shocked embarrassment when Jesus put the request for baptism to him (Matthew 3:14–16).

If Jesus had also confided to John not merely his destiny but the way that he himself interpreted kingship, then other matters are explained. The word "Messiah," in the minds of all who knew the truth, meant neither more nor less than king. Such men would have foreseen a royal destiny for Jesus, ruling from a colourful court, surrounded by armed and faithful guards, by splendid courtiers, and himself clad in the glorious robes of earthly kingship. Though such was the view of others, the task of the Anointed One, as Jesus was to interpret it, was not to govern any visible kingdom. It was rather to lead his people and through them the world back to the worship of their one God and to reveal to them new aspects of that God's compassion and forgiveness. Where John preached that past sins could be washed away in the cool waters of Jordan, Jesus showed a gentler and yet a sterner way. He saw the task of the Anointed One as acting as the scapegoat of the world, the surrogate sacrifice of all mankind, washing away not only past but all future sins by the lamblike sacrifice of his own blood.

Had he confided in John not merely the purpose but

the style of his future mission, then many of John's words fall easily into place: "I baptise you with water but there is one who cometh after me who shall baptise you with fire." It was through the fire of suffering and pain that Jesus was to baptise the world. "Behold the Lamb of God." John, without hesitation and as if he already knew of Jesus' intentions, saw him at the first encounter by the banks of the Jordan as the scapegoat of ancient ritual and the world's sacrificial lamb for a new and universal passover.

# 8

# We Have Found the Messias

As soon as Jesus emerged as a public figure, there were many who were sure that he was the Messiah. Even as he walked away from the River Jordan, after being acclaimed and baptised by John, two of the latter's disciples, one of whom was Simon Peter's brother, Andrew, followed him. They asked him where he lived, and he invited them to follow him back to his own home. They did so, and Andrew forthwith went out to find his brother, Simon Peter, and told him quite unambiguously, "We have found the Messias" (John 1:37–41).

That John's two disciples should have at once recognised him as the Messiah and that Andrew should so eagerly have told his brother is in itself not highly significant. After all, many had thought that John the

Baptist was himself the Anointed One; the expectation of the coming of the promised king was once more alive. It is not surprising therefore that many wondered whether, and some were sure that, Jesus the new teacher was the promised leader.

It is far more significant that Jesus himself accepted the truth of this identification very early and publicly declared himself to be the expected Messiah. After his first teaching in Judea he left that province and travelled to Galilee. To do so he had to pass through Samaria and stop at a Samaritan city called Sychar. He rested there by a well, reputed to be Jacob's Well, wearied by his journey and thirsty in the hot sunshine. A Samaritan woman came to the well, and he asked her for water to drink. She was surprised by this, for the people of Judea and the Samaritans were by no means friendly. She fell into conversation with Jesus and they discussed how God ought to be worshipped. They also discussed where such worship should be given, for the Samaritans did not visit Jerusalem to take part in the Temple rites but worshipped God on a mountainside in their own country. She brushed aside Jesus' arguments and implied that he had no authority to lay down the law. She said she knew that the Messias was coming and that when he appeared, 'He will tell us all things.' To her immense surprise, Jesus told her very specifically that he himself was the Messiah (John 4:26).

Two important points emerge: First, Jesus was seen as the Messiah immediately after his baptism and before he had gathered together all his twelve followers; second, he himself did not merely refrain from denying that he was the Anointed One, but volunteered the information to a woman who was a total stranger. The questions which were pressed home so forcefully at his trials were not directed to securing an admission that he was the Messiah. That was well known. Their purpose was rather to discover what was his own interpretation of the role—political kingship or spiritual leadership. The first was an offence to the Romans, the second an affront to the Jewish establishment.

The promised figure of the Anointed One meant different things to different people, for the prophecies were as diverse as they were numerous. But to all men its origins were clear. And those origins were regal, connected with the ancient kingdom of David. So from the start of his ministry Jesus was accepted as, and at Jacob's Well declared himself to be, some kind of king of the Jewish nation.

But precisely what kind of king had his contemporaries in mind? For many of them the expected Messiah would be a warlike figure who would reestablish David's kingdom by force of arms. All men knew that Saul, the first anointed king of Israel, was appointed by Samuel to lead his people in victorious war. Now the times of Saul had come again. As in his day, Israel was now beset by many foes. She lay under the domination, not of the Philistines and other neighbouring tribes but of Rome's great military machine.

As Saul had fought manfully against the enemies of Israel and as David had organised his people under captains to march against their many foes, so would his descendant—the long-awaited king—lead his people from the tyranny of the Herodian family and the oppression of Rome's alien power.

For the Zealots and for those who remembered the gallant resistance of Judas the Galilean and the bitter cruelties inflicted upon his defeated followers, it was assuredly the new king's warlike aspects to which they eagerly looked forward. They saw him as the leader of a resistance movement which would drive the Romans out of the land of Israel forever, who would cleanse the city of Jerusalem and the hill of Zion from the pagan armies which now oppressed God's people, and who would once more bring under his holy sceptre all the lands over which David had once ruled, including Syria to the north, where now the proud Roman governor lay. The road would not be easy, nor would the journey towards final victory be without its setbacks. Years ago the prophet Daniel had foretold that there should be war and desolation, that the city of Jerusalem and even the holy sanctuary would be destroyed. The Messiah, the promised king, would have to fight nearly two years before he triumphed:

> Know therefore and understand that from the going forth of the commandment to restore and to build Jerusalem unto the Messiah the Prince shall be seven weeks, and three score and two weeks: the street shall be built again, and the wall, even in troublous times.
>
> And after three score and two weeks shall Messiah be cut off, but not for himself: and the people of the Prince that shall come shall destroy the city and the sanctuary: and the end thereof shall be with a flood, and unto the end of the war desolations are determined (Daniel 9:25–26).

If Matthew is to be believed, it was these expectations

of a warrior prince which were dominant even at the time of Jesus' birth. Herod called his priests and learned men together to find out whether the promised prince had been born. They said to him, "And thou Bethlehem, in the land of Juda, are not the least among the princes of Juda: for out of thee shall come a Governor that shall rule my people Israel" (Matthew 2:6).

But the word "Governor" does not truly reflect the words in the version of the Gospels used by the early church. About the year A.D. 400 Saint Jerome translated the Bible into Latin for the use of the common people. This version, known as the Vulgate, was drawn up at a time when the imperial system still survived and when men were still familiar with the titles, both civil and military, of imperial officers. It is therefore very significant that the words of Matthew are given in the Vulgate as *Ex te enim exiet dux qui regat populum meum,* that is to say, "Out of thee there shall come a military commander who shall govern my people Israel." The word *dux* meant originally the commander of a group of armies—often of an expeditionary force. Later, commanders came to be stationed permanently in the different provinces, and the word came to mean both a military commander and the head of a military administration. The English word "duke" derives from it. Saint Jerome's use of this term strongly suggests that those who expected the coming of the new king were anticipating the advent of a great military leader under whom the people of Israel would sweep forward to victory.

This was the role which many saw Jesus as fulfilling.

They yearned for the day when this new preacher would cast off his peaceful robes, buckle on his armour, draw his sword, and lead his warlike people through the clamour and ardours of battle. For Jesus these expectations were an impediment to the greater tasks which he had set himself. But the expectations were urgently present, and there were many pressures seeking to impel him towards violence.

So, through the word *dux,* we begin to see Jesus through the eyes of his contemporaries as a warrior king—keeping his plans and purposes secret from the all-powerful enemy of Rome but destined one day to announce himself, to wear helmet and breastplate, and to lead forth his armies as his great ancestor David had once done. By the time that Saint Jerome was writing there were permanent garrisons in numerous provinces, each commanded by a *dux* who represented the armed might of the Caesars. There was a duke of Britain, a duke of Spain, a duke of Cyrenaica, and many more. The legendary King Arthur, who flourished shortly after Saint Jerome was writing, was almost certainly such a one—the duke of Britain. It is strange to see the figure of Jesus through the eyes of those who, in his lifetime, saw him as the potential Duke of Judea, a splendid armoured figure moving resolutely against the Roman legions.

What Jesus said did little to dispel, and by misunderstanding often seemed to reinforce, the warlike hopes of his more militant listeners. He continually used the metaphor of God's kingdom to explain his purpose. To the spiritually devout the kingdom of God was a manner of expressing a situation in which men would eschew all sin and in which God's will would utterly prevail. God would rule like a king over a cleansed world, inhabited by men grown totally virtuous and totally pious.

But to those of angry heart and to those who knew the sorrowful history of their people it would have meant something quite different. It was the visible and physical kingdom of David which was the kingdom of God, for God had a covenant with Israel; his strength and compassion had ruled and protected the kingdom through his servant David. To such the parable of the kingdom was a promise that Jesus, a descendant of David, would assume the sacred but real kingship over the people of Israel under the direct guidance of God.

They knew he could not speak openly, for should his intentions become clear to the Roman authorities, his days would be numbered. He would be seized for sedition and meet the savage fate that had befallen all other rebels against Rome. Too early a disclosure of his royal and warlike plans would cast over his bright armour the dreadful shadow of the cross, for it was on the cross that Rome hanged her rebels and her slaves—the cross on which death came slowly, not through any clean and mortal wound, but as a welcome end to days of torment, exposure, weariness, and intolerable pain.

So the very ambiguity of the parables of the kingdom supported the view of the militants. Why did Jesus so continually use the metaphor of the coming kingdom if he were not trying to tell them, as openly as he dared, that he would lead them as Judas the Galilean had led them—but this time to the final predestined victory?

Had his intentions been otherwise, there were other metaphors available to explain the new revelation of God. There was the imagery which his great forebear, David, had used to describe God as the guardian and shepherd of his people. Jesus did indeed use such turns of phrase, which came naturally to him and his listeners alike. Each hillside and village had its flock of sheep and goats, and to the vast multitude of his listeners the shepherd was a far more usual sight than a king! But it was the kingdom that he preached far more often than the conception of the divine shepherd.

The events of Palm Sunday bear witness to his general acceptance as the king of Israel. For the welcome he received that day in Jerusalem was a royal welcome. The crowd gave him the traditional royal salutation of "Hosanna," an ancient Hebrew word meaning "praise to the high one." The greeting was not addressed to God but addressed directly to Jesus, for we are told that the crowd called out, "Hosanna to the Son of David" (Matthew 21:9). He was hailed explicitly as the king, for the crowd shouted, "Blessed is the king of Israel that cometh in the name of the lord" (John 12:13). And his entering into Jerusalem riding upon a young ass was seen in John's Gospel as a fulfilment of an ancient and royal prophecy: ". . . thy king cometh into thee: and riding upon an ass and upon a colt the foal of an ass" (Zechariah, 9:9). That particular prophecy was significant because it was set in a military context.

It is not difficult to imagine the excitement that ran through the city when the news of the king's arrival spread through the narrow streets. It spread swiftly among the city's own inhabitants and among the thronging visitors who had come from distant villages and towns to celebrate the feast of the Passover in the holy city. All those who had seen Jesus as the conquering king of the prophecies were now thrilled with the expectation that the blow was about to be struck for freedom and that their royal commander had come to lead them.

This tragic misunderstanding lies behind the extraordinary change in the crowd's attitudes between Palm Sunday and Good Friday. On Sunday Jesus was greeted enthusiastically as king, with the crowd casting their garments before him and cheering him so that the streets rang with their shouts. On Friday they were clamouring for his crucifixion. Frustrated in their high and mistaken expectations, the city mob changed its shouts of admiration to yells of execration in a few brief days. Mingled with the bitter disappointment that their king was not after all their leader in war, there would have been a great and growing anger against him. If the promised king's prophesied mission was a martial one, his failure to lead them in war was proof that he was but a false Messiah. By what right had he come riding on the colt of an ass? By what right had he accepted the plaudits of a king, given so dangerously under the eyes of the Romans? He had deceived the people! Betrayal to the Romans and the cruellest of Roman deaths was the least he deserved.

There was another conception of the Messiah which the less militant of his listeners might have sought in Jesus. This was the Anointed One as the great reviver of the faith—the one who would call the nation of Israel back to the true worship of God, unifying the people and putting an end to the schisms that divided sect from sect. Such was the figure which the Samaritan woman by Jacob's Well was expecting. Such a one would represent no cause for anxiety to the Roman authorities. Far from fomenting revolt or from secretly plotting to lead the nation in arms against the invaders, such a one would be concerned only with religious truth. He would be the Prince of Peace foretold in Isaiah's prophecy.

But though he would not have incurred the wrath of the Romans, he would certainly have come into conflict with the Jewish authorities. Herod the Tetrarch could not have welcomed him, since such an Anointed One would be a claimant to the leadership of the Jews. Nor would the priesthood and the Levites welcome any such intruder into the field of their own authority. Just as they had asked John the Baptist by what authority he was acting, so they would have jealously challenged any Messiah who appeared in the guise of a purely religious teacher. The Zealots too would have rejected such a man of peace as failing in the national duty of defiance of Rome's alien power.

There must have been many of his followers who saw Jesus in this light, for a great deal of what he taught was consistent with this more peaceful role. He enjoined his followers to love their neighbours. And he went out of his way to teach that even one's enemies were neighbours in the context of that injunction. It was a Samaritan who was the centre of the parable of the man who fell among thieves. It was not the Levites and not even the Judeans who were depicted as true neighbours of the injured man, for they passed by on the other side. It was the Samaritan—a man from a nation who was traditionally at enmity with the Judeans—who fulfilled the role of a neighbour in Jesus' definition.

On other occasions he was more explicit, instructing his followers to love their enemies and to do good to those who hated them. In the political context of the society within which he was teaching, the natural enemies were the Romans. As some took his parables of the kingdom as indications of secret rebellion, so others could have interpreted these new injunctions as signs that he had laid aside patriotism and was content to forgive and indeed to appease the national enemy. Thus even in his role of Prince of Peace he could not, in the contemporary political context, escape the odium of some of the people.

There was one further definition of the Messiah which, in the eyes of at least some of his followers, Jesus satisfied. This was the prophecy of Isaiah, that the Messiah would be "the Mighty Everlasting God, the Father, the Prince of Peace" (Isaiah 9:6). In other words, the coming Messiah would be not only king of Israel but would himself be the embodiment of Israel's God. Much of what Jesus said and did could be so interpreted. It was usual for prophets and teachers to say what they said in the name of God. They did not arrogate to themselves the power to instruct but were content to be the instruments through which God made his purposes known. Moses reported he had heard God's voice on the mountainside and declared that the laws he brought down had been engraved by God himself upon the tablets. But frequently Jesus spoke directly and said what he had to say in his own person without ascribing his teachings to any higher power. To many this could mean only that he saw himself as the Most High and was by implication claiming to be a personification of God himself.

But such an implied claim, unless proven beyond all doubt and supported by the kind of miracle to which the Jewish people had been accustomed in their Scriptures—a voice from heaven, the collapse of a city's walls, the arresting of the sun in the sky—might be nothing more than the blasphemous rantings of an arrogant or deranged man.

So Jesus was caught in a trap with three entrances. If he were the Messiah, as he himself had claimed, then he was the predestined king of Israel and, if a warlike king, doomed to be put down by the Roman power; if he were the Prince of Peace, sincerely preaching abstention from all violence and the positive giving of love and affection to one's enemies, then he was bound to attract the execration of the more militantly patriotic of the Jews in general and of the Zealots in particular. Finally, if he saw his Messiahship as making him the mighty God, the everlasting Father, then he was bound to be ostracised by the priesthood and his mission doomed to end in temporal failure in which he himself would suffer a criminal's death which was the blasphemer's due.

# 9

# Imperial Sons of God

Even if Jesus could have escaped from the triple trap which the Messianic prophecy had set for him, there was yet a fourth political peril into which he could fall. This was the claim advanced by some of his followers that he was the Son of God. The first appearance of this is to be found in Matthew's account of his baptism: "And lo a voice from heaven saying this is my beloved Son in whom I am well pleased" (Matthew 3:17). At his trial (which we shall consider later) the high priest demanded of Jesus not only whether he was the Anointed One but whether he was the Son of God (Matthew 26:63). It is true that the claim reached its fullest maturity only after Christ's death. But the instances quoted are enough to show that it was current during his lifetime.

The claim poses several questions to the sceptical mind: first, why was it not laughed out of court, as such a claim might well be today? Second, what historic circumstances had rendered acceptable the idea that a man could indeed be the Son of God? Finally why, although rationally acceptable, was such an idea politically repugnant to the provincial authorities? For an answer to all these questions we must turn to Rome's history during the sixty years which preceded the Crucifixion.

For more than four centuries Rome had execrated the name and title of king. The state had originally been a monarchy, and Livy gives an account, half legend and half history, of Rome's early kings. They were divinely descended. They held absolute power over their people, guiding their subjects not only in matters temporal but in matters spiritual. They were the intermediaries between mortal men and the immortal gods. But Tarquin, the last of these legendary kings, had been arrogant and tyrannous. The climax came when, believing himself above the law, he had raped Lucrece, the wife of one of his generals. Out of humiliation and shame she had stabbed herself, after first summoning her kinsfolk and telling them of the king's hideous act. Led by Brutus (ancestor of that Brutus who was friend to the great Julius Caesar some four hundred years later), the Romans cast out Tarquin, put an end to the institution of monarchy, and resolved never to tolerate another king.

But they recognised that the institution of kingship was pleasing to the gods and that only a king could intercede with the immortals on their behalf. Yet even this deeply felt religious view did not diminish their hatred of temporal kings or tempt them to restore the monarchy. Instead they appointed an officer who had the title of *rex sacrorum*—the King of Holy Matters. With the name but without any of the powers of a monarch, he could discharge the sacred rites that required a king's presence and speak to the gods on the people's behalf, but Rome herself became a republic. Such was the hatred for the very name of king that it was enacted that any man who plotted to assume the monarchy should suffer death.

As a check against the renewal of tyranny, the republic was governed by two elected magistrates (the consuls), each with equal powers and each able to veto the other. Inevitably conflicts arose and civil war ensued. Some forty years before the birth of Jesus, Julius Caesar (then consul) was assassinated on the mere suspicion that he was planning a revival of the monarchy. He had arrogated to himself all powers in the state, wore every day the golden wreath which his triumphs had won for him and which so dangerously resembled a royal crown, and he appeared daily in the Senate in the triumphal robes which were so close to the royal vestments of former days. Caesar's blood, which his assassins spilled ruthlessly on the marble floor of the Senate house, was renewed evidence of the hatred of the Roman state for any monarch. And this despite the fact that Caesar had healed the wounds that had torn the state apart, had put an end to the interminable civil wars fought between consul and consul, and had brought new and wider lands under the proud sway of Rome's eagles.

After his death there were long wars between his assassins on the one hand and his friends on the other, and it was the latter who finally emerged victorious. Among them was Julius' great-nephew Octavius, grandson of his sister Julia, who was only nineteen years old at the time of Julius' murder. When the latter's will was read, it was disclosed that he had posthumously adopted Octavius as his son. Octavius accordingly took the family name of Caesar, seized power in the state, and later was awarded the title of Augustus. This is the Caesar Augustus who ended the republic, who founded the empire, and in whose reign Jesus was born.

After young Caesar's final victory and emergence as the new power in Rome, steps were taken to reinstate Julius' reputation and to honour his memory. As a permanent memorial the Senate named the month of July after him. The Senate further declared that his spirit had been received by Jove, the divine father, as one of the gods. Temples were built to his divinity and an order of priesthood appointed.

Four years after the Battle of Actium, at which the last of his enemies were defeated, young Caesar was given the name of Augustus—the revered one. With the awful example of Julius before him, he did not dare, even at the height of his popularity, to claim the title of king. He was content with the honorific of Augustus and with the informal title of *princeps,* or first citizen.

He had no precise legal right to the supreme position which he now held. His only claim, and it was a slender one, was that he was the adopted son of the now-deified Julius Caesar, to whose golden days people now looked back with longing as days of peace and firm government.

The only means of propaganda at Augustus' disposal was the coinage, which circulated in all the lands from the Atlantic to the Danube and from the North Sea to the gleaming cities of Africa. So upon this abundant coinage he declared himself to be *Augustus divi filius*—Augustus, Son of the God. Neither the definite nor the indefinite article was in frequent use in Latin, and the words *divi filius* could equally be interpreted more briefly as Augustus, Son of God. The different folk who made up the empire could interpret the words in their own different ways. Those who believed in many gods could take them at their face value, that Augustus was the son of the new god, Julius. The Jews, who believed in one God, could take them in the same way, as an arrogant pagan claim, or they could take them as a blasphemous suggestion that the emperor was the son of the one true God.

Augustus lived to a great age, dying in A.D. 14. Thus it was that for many decades coins bearing this inscription circulated throughout the empire. Men became familiar with the conception that the great emperor who ruled them and whose stern troops they saw daily in their own cities and countryside was the son of some divine being.

Nor did the matter end there. Towards the end of his reign Augustus was in considerable doubt as to how to arrange the succession. He had no surviving sons and had arranged for his daughter Julia to marry his great general, Agrippa, whom he thus designated his heir. But Agrippa died, as did his two sons, Augustus' grandchildren, so that the plans and hopes of Caesar Augustus came to naught. He then arranged for Julia to marry his stepson, Tiberius, son of his wife Livia by an earlier marriage. This marriage now marked Tiberius out as his successor, but to make the situation even clearer to the peoples of the empire, he formally adopted Tiberius as his son. So now Tiberius, like Augustus before him, took the family name Caesar and became Tiberius Caesar. Again Augustus made use of the coinage as a medium of propaganda. He struck three coins bearing Tiberius' portrait and declaring the latter to be *Augusti filius imperatoris*—Son of Augustus the Emperor.

After Augustus died, the Senate paid him the same honours which had been granted to his great-uncle Julius. They named the month of August after him. Like Julius, he was deified by the Senate, became officially a god, had temples raised to his divinity and priests appointed to conduct his worship. Thus Tiberius on his accession was, like Augustus, the son of a god and, like Augustus, proudly proclaimed it upon his coinage. So by the time Jesus began his ministry, the people of Judea had been accustomed, for as long as men could remember, to see emperors described as sons of a divine power. Two generations at least had come to accept this.

So by the time of Jesus, the conception that a mortal man could be the son of God was neither novel nor unacceptable. But (and here was the further political jeopardy into which Jesus was placed) to claim such divine origins—or to permit one's followers to make the claim on one's behalf—was to set oneself up as an equal of the emperor and would have appeared to the Roman authorities as an arrogant and seditious usurpation of imperial power. Maybe it was the knowledge that such a claim amounted to a challenge to Tiberius Caesar's personal authority which prompted the high priest to ask Jesus at his trial whether he was the Son of God or no.

What was a matter of deadly personal peril to Jesus proved to be both a stimulant and a danger to the infant church. It stimulated the growth of the faith since the practice of deifying emperors continued after the death of Tiberius. Thus the central theme of the young church, that Christ was the Son of God, was a not-unacceptable conception to all the people dwelling within the empire. Yet it was at the same time a grave peril, for coupled with the early Christians' strict monotheism, which prevented them (as it had prevented their predecessors, the Jews) from worshipping the divinity of the emperor, it brought on the Christians the rigour of persecution. They denied the emperor's divinity, but believed in the numinous quality of their dead leader.

The Roman coinage is mentioned twice in the Gospels—once by implication and once explicitly. When Judea became a Roman province, all men had to pay two taxes—the traditional national tax to the Temple for the support of the priesthood and to meet the cost of the rites and the ceremonies of worship and a second tax to the Roman imperial treasury to defray the costs of the civil and military administration. The temple tax was paid in the traditional coin of Israel, the shekel, since Roman coinage was unacceptable for this purpose.

No one could bring into the Temple treasury coins which, in breach of the Second Commandment, bore images of the emperors and of the allegorical figures which so often appeared on the reverse. But when pilgrims came to the Temple from places far afield for the feast of the Passover or for the celebrations of the Day of Atonement, they would have brought with them, not the traditional Jewish coinage but the much commoner Roman coins, which were now the common currency of the marketplace. Before they could buy the doves or lambs for the sacrifice or pay their temple dues, they had to change their bronze sesterces or silver denarii, both bearing the image of the emperor, for the traditional shekel. So in the outer courtyard of the Temple the money changers had set up their tables and laid out their boxes of coins. These were the tables which Jesus overturned. They were performing a necessary function in exchanging the common but ritually unacceptable money into coinage which could enter the Temple itself without any affront to tradition.

The other mention of Roman coinage is more precise. We have seen how some men took Jesus as a secret rebel against Rome while others saw him as unpatriotically appeasing the foreign power. His enemies resolved to force him into defining his political position by asking him outright whether the people should continue to pay their taxes to the Roman authorities. His answer is well known. He called for someone from the crowd to hand him a coin. A denarius, no doubt of Tiberius, was handed up to him. He drew the crowd's attention to Caesar's portrait on the coin, which clearly marked the piece with Caesar's ownership. He then told the crowd that they should give back to Caesar what was already Caesar's and should give to God what was God's. The reply could cause offence to neither party. His words could mean quite simply that it was proper to pay the Roman taxes in Roman money and the temple dues in Jewish shekels.

But the underlying importance of the Roman coinage was that it spread the idea, as a commonplace in shop and tavern, in pottery and smithy, in vineyard and marketplace, that the distant emperor was the son of a god. The proud boast of Augustus, which he ordered his mints to place on his coinage, showing him to be the heir and adopted son of the dead and now-divine Julius, and the continuation of this tradition by Tiberius all helped to create a climate in which Jesus, the Messiah, could be seen without incredulity and within the spirit of the age as the Son of God.

# 10

# The Visible Kingdom Renounced

Almost immediately after his baptism Jesus went into the wilderness for a period of fasting and meditation. He was, in effect, repeating what John had already done. He, like Jesus, had spent some time away from the habitations of men as a prelude to his own public preaching.

We do not know what visions John saw during the long days and nights when nothing more than a coarse camel's-hair cloak protected him against the heat of the sun and the chill of the dark. Nor is there either record or inference of the inner problems he had to resolve before he felt ready for his journey to Jordan and for his vehement preaching of the need for a universal repentance. In the case of Jesus, however, we have sure knowledge of the problems with which he had to wrestle and the hard decisions he had to take before embarking on his own ministry.

We know, from his conversation with the Samaritan woman by Jacob's Well, that he knew himself to be the Messiah, the rightful king of Israel. Moreover, this awareness stood high in his consciousness, or he would not have shared his knowledge so readily with a complete stranger. Knowing himself to be the rightful heir of the Davidic dynasty and destined by ancient prophecies to be successful in any attempts he might make to take the throne, he had a tormenting decision to make. Was he to interpret the secret with which his parents had entrusted him as a duty to fulfil the angry wishes of many of the people, driving out both the Herodian rulers and the Romans? Or was he to take up the other role of the Messiah and become the spiritual rather than the temporal leader of his people, preaching the invisible kingdom of God rather than the revived kingdom of David?

Traditionally the place in the wilderness to which Jesus retreated to resolve these problems is the mountain known as the Mount of Temptation, on which today there now stands a Greek Orthodox monastery. It lies to the north of the Dead Sea, to one side of the Jericho road in the Jordan valley. The tradition makes good geographical sense, for after his baptism we know that Jesus journeyed southwards from the Lake of Galilee along the Jordan valley and through Samaria. Such a journey, continued southwards, would have brought him very close to the Mount of Temptation.

From the top of the hill much of the kingdom is

visible. Behind the peak there gauntly stand the waterless mountains of Judea, bearing neither grass nor tree. But southwards there is a clear view across the still waters of the Dead Sea to Mount Pisgah and northwards to Mount Hermon. It was from this mountain that Moses, after the long journey from Egypt, saw the promised land of Canaan. And it was in a nearby valley that his unknown sepulchre was said to have been placed. To the south lay the fortress of Macherus, standing upon rising ground. In this stronghold, according to Josephus, John the Baptist was beheaded.

All this and much more was visible to Jesus during the forty days of his retreat. Not far away lay the city of Jericho and, farther westwards, Jerusalem itself and the village of Bethany, which he knew so well. And south of Jerusalem lay the small town of Bethlehem, where he had been born. It was a fine vantage point from which a prince of David's house could see the magnificence of his inheritance. Here he could gain a true measure of the temptation to make a bid for all territorial splendour, to let the plan of mere religious leadership blow away on the dusty desert wind.

We do not have to believe in the physical appearance of a personal devil who came to him and who showed him, from that vantage point, the riches of the earthly kingdom. Certainly the forces of ambition and of selfishness, the desire for royal raiment, a proud court, and sovereignty over his fellowmen must all have been present. And if the narrators of the scene chose to personify those forces and to describe the presence of a devil, then they were being no more than the children of their own age.

The temptation itself was real enough, and the conflict between aspirations towards temporal or spiritual leadership was as urgent as it was agonising. To be king of the visible kingdom would be a fine thing, and the old prophecies were sufficient assurance that he could achieve the throne of his fathers. But he put the temptation behind him and with it any lingering plans he may have had to be a second and more successful Judas of Galilee, a leader of the Zealots, a military king, rather than simply a religious teacher.

The decision taken on the Mount of Temptation was crucial to his ministry and has always been recognized as such. Hermits and holy men, from as early as the third century, have inhabited caves and cells upon the mountainside, hoping, if they made their dwellings close to that enchanted place, that they could share in the experience of Jesus, cast aside all earthly temptations, and lead a life consistent with that taught by their master.

Thereafter, sure of his purpose and knowing which of the diverse roles of the expected Messiah he would fulfil, he embarked on the great adventure of his ministry. Soon after he began his public teaching, news of Jesus was taken to Herod. This shows that Jesus quickly made sufficient stir for the tetrarch's agents to make report of the matter. We have already noted Herod's startling reaction—his question whether the new teacher was not John the Baptist come again.

Since his appearance as a public figure was quickly reported to Herod, we may infer that it was also reported to the Roman authorities and that Pilate too would have heard something of his early activities.

From all that we have already seen of Pilate, it is clear that he was particularly sensitive to the religious fervour (or fanaticism, as he saw it) of the stubborn people he governed. He would therefore have learned with some apprehension of the appearance of a new religious leader. Only a little while before, that other teacher, John the Baptist, had engendered a dangerous revival of religious enthusiasm. Pilate, like Herod in the account of Josephus, might have seen in John a potential rebel and a threat to Rome's authority. He would have learned of John's execution with particular satisfaction. The execution of a notable Jewish religious teacher by a Jewish ruler was a welcome sign of disunity among the subject people. Tacitus was to write some years later (putting the words into the mouth of a defiant British leader on the eve of battle) that Rome's method of ruling the nations she had conquered was to foster divisions among them—*divide et impera*—divide and rule. Herod, in executing John, had proved a perfect example of Rome's system and had carried out his task with classical precision.

So on the first news of Jesus' appearance, just as Herod had seen him as John the Baptist come again, Pilate might have considered him as yet another potential troublemaker, secretly hoping that Herod would once more solve the problem without involving Rome. But Pilate would soon have learned that he had little cause for fear. Jesus was neither moving the people to rebellion nor challenging Rome's authority.

Immediately after the temptation, when Jesus made his final and irrevocable decision not to pursue any claim to a temporal kingdom, Matthew reports him as having been accepted as a teacher in the synagogues of Galilee. He healed many people, and great multitudes flocked to him from Galilee, from Jerusalem, from Judea, and from beyond Jordan. His fame spread northwards into Syria, so that Pilate's superior, the governor of Syria, would also have heard of the new figure who had so suddenly appeared on the Jewish scene (Matthew 4:23–25).

Immediately thereafter Matthew (5, 6, and 7) reports him as having given his first sustained oration to the crowds. It is of such length and complexity that it seems improbable that Matthew is claiming to give a verbatim report of one single speech. More probably the Sermon on the Mount represents a careful summary by Matthew of all the main teachings of Jesus, put together with great skill for the benefit of future ages. It falls into several distinct parts, each of which may represent one aspect of the lessons which Jesus taught at different times to the eager crowds. None of them could have caused the least alarm to Pilate or his officers.

The first section, known as the Beatitudes, is an unambiguous call to the Jewish people to accept poverty, sorrow, and oppression without thought of defiance. It was men of peace who would be blessed, not men of violence. It was a challenge to the whole philosophy of the Zealot movement and to their belief in armed force as an instrument of patriotism and religious resurgence.

Such teaching would have been welcome both to Pilate and to the Roman authorities at large. Here was a moderate man who had a massive following, who was preaching submission to Rome's rule in terms as clear as the national political climate permitted. Not only was he commending patience and peace to his followers, he was exhorting them to accept persecution and to bear all manner of evil.

In the next clear section of the Sermon on the Mount, representing another aspect of his teaching, Jesus made it clear that he saw himself as an Orthodox Jew teaching Jews: "Think not that I am come to destroy the Law, or the prophets: I am not come to destroy, but to fulfil" (Matthew 5:17). The section continues with a commentary on the Commandments. It would have shown to the Roman authorities that Jesus was seeking no political power but setting himself up as a fervent supporter, albeit a reformer, of the Jewish religion. If he was seeking any controversy, it was with the "scribes and Pharisees" rather than with the political authorities of the state. The section ends with a further exhortation to patience and to nonviolence, culminating in the specific command: "Love your enemies, bless them that curse you, do good to them that hate you, and pray for them which despitefully use you and persecute you" (Matthew 5:44). For the majority of Jews the word "enemies" could mean only, apart from a few neighbours and acquaintances with whom they might have some petty personal quarrels, the Roman officials, police, and soldiers. So here again his teachings were, from the Roman point of view, unexceptionable.

The third section of the Sermon (Matthew 6) shows Jesus explaining the new relationship which he advocated between the Jewish people and their God. For their good deeds God's approbation was sufficient. They were not to seek the praise of their fellowmen when they gave alms, fasted, or did other good works. It was enough for God to see their righteousness. Nor were they to be ambitious for wealth or possessions. This, in Roman eyes, was preaching an acceptable kind of stoicism. A people who followed such a leader would be in no mood for rebellion. The more his message spread, the better. It would make the task of the Zealots and the troublesome militants far more difficult should they ever again attempt to raise the standard of revolt against the Roman power.

The central message of this section was the lesson he gave to the people as to how they should pray. They were to address their God as Father. They were to ask him for no more than their daily bread, forgiveness of their sins (just as they would forgive all who sinned against them), and freedom from the temptation of committing any evil act.

The final section of his teaching (Matthew 7) was a further exhortation to righteousness and a further statement of their God's essential compassion. It also contained a denunciation of men who, under the guise of religion, were preaching false doctrines. Many of his listeners might have interpreted this as referring to the militants, who, by appealing to the Jewish faith and patriotism, had so often persuaded the people to take up arms against Rome and to suffer the inevitable and cruel punishment. He said, "Beware of false prophets, which come to you in sheep's clothing, but inward they are ravening wolves" (Matthew 7:15 and 16). As a tree was known by its fruit, so was a prophet known by the fruits of his preaching. Thorns and thistles were all the fruits which the tree of false prophecy could bear.

Again the Romans could have had no quarrel with such a doctrine. Even if Jesus were not deliberately referring to the Zealot party, certainly he could be taken as doing so. Here was a man of peace, a Jew calling the Jews back to the ancient purity of their religion, but doing so peacefully and warning them against following every rabble-rouser who appeared.

Certainly there was nothing to arouse the hostility of Pilate or of the soldiers and officials whose task it was to maintain Rome's peace in the province of Judea. Yet there was one aspect of his teaching which would have puzzled them and which ultimately was to form the basis for his conviction before a Roman court.

# 11

# The Growing Enmity

The Romans were as concerned with supporting the authority of the tetrarchs they had set up over the Jews as with maintaining their own power. Indeed, the fragmentation of the Jewish nation into several provinces, each under its local ruler, was one of the main instruments whereby Roman authority was exercised. The continued existence of these compliant native monarchs was a guarantee of Rome's security. Pilate and the authorities generally accepted the most outrageous and depraved behavior on the part of these client rulers, provided that they remained loyal to Caesar and his representatives. They could be offered cynical flattery and all the outward show of power. They could give full rein to the most vicious cruelty and caprice, and Rome would raise no objections. Herod the

Great could slaughter all the children of a region and this was not seen as any breach of the majesty of Rome's peace. Herod the Tetrarch, his son, could order the execution of the prophet John. So long as a watchdog is obedient, alert, and totally dependent, no sensible master will raise too many questions about the savagery of its behavior. For Pilate, therefore, the Zealots who directly challenged Rome's military power were no more dangerous than nationalist leaders who challenged the authority of her puppet rulers.

Jesus' continued references to "the kingdom" were thus as unwelcome to the Roman authorities as they were puzzling. Before he had, by his own life and death, endowed the word "Messiah" with a share in the supreme divinity, it meant neither more nor less than the anointed king of the Jews. And if his declaration that he was the Messiah (for example, at Jacob's Well) had been reported to the prefect, it would have been couched in just those terms. It must have been common knowledge that this man was of the house of David, for Joseph neither would nor could have made any secret of what was always a public administrative fact. Therefore Jesus' declaration that he was the Anointed One posed a serious threat to Herod. And when in his teaching he continually referred to a kingdom, Roman suspicions must also have been aroused despite the overtly pacific nature of his teachings.

The Romans, a matter-of-fact and unfanciful nation, were not likely to have understood Jesus' method of teaching abstract conceptions by means of concrete narratives. Nor were they aware of the two kingdoms—

the visible and the invisible—the memory of which lay deep in the collective subconscious of the Jewish people.

Of the first they certainly knew. The reigns of the great kings David and Solomon were well recorded and were no doubt familiar to the Roman provincial officials whose business it was to learn all they could about the people over whom they ruled. But the invisible kingdom—the abstract symbol of Jewish religious independence and of the people's hope to see a revival of God's direct authority—lay beyond their mental grasp.

As we have seen, they could not equate the Jewish God with any of their own divinities or understand his spiritual and disembodied mysteries. Therefore, to the extent that they learned that Jesus was preaching about the kingdom of this incomprehensible God and teaching his followers specifically to pray for the establishment of that kingdom on earth, his message would have seemed perilously close to sedition. His words could mean only one thing: a direct challenge to the authority of Rome's chosen Jewish rulers and therefore to the authority of Rome itself.

The parables of Jesus were varied, but his references to the kingdom were constant and unchanging. Matthew records that this concept lay at the heart of his teaching early in his ministry, when he was visiting the synagogues and when he was travelling throughout Galilee healing the sick (Matthew 4:23). Matthew is not reporting one single message which Jesus conveyed to his followers, but tells us of his ceaseless reference to this theme: "And Jesus went about all Galilee, teaching in their synagogues, and preaching the doctrine of the kingdom . . . " (Matthew 4:23). The same conception recurred in the prayer which Jesus taught his followers in the Sermon on the Mount as reported by Matthew. After the salutation to God as the universal Father the idea of the kingdom stands at the very head of the prayer. In fact it was therefore the universal authority of God rather than a kingdom in the earthly sense that Jesus was preaching to his followers.

It is clear that even his devoted followers found the conception of the kingdom a subtle and difficult one. The many explanations which Jesus gave of it indicate how often he must have been asked what he meant by it. He likened the kingdom to many things and to many situations—to a grain of mustard seed, to a man sowing, to a man building a house. If the doctrine was difficult for his own adherents to understand, how much more difficult must it have been for the unsympathetic Roman authorities? They would not have been disposed to waste time on philosophical or historical analyses of the words reported to them. It was enough for them that here was a man preaching a kingdom which was different from, and seemingly promoted in defiance of, the established social and political order. Since it was known that he was a prince (from however impoverished a branch) of the ancient royal house, was he cryptically proposing himself as a candidate for a revived Jewish monarchy? Such ideas clearly represented a grave danger to the state. The perils of such a claim outweighed the apparently pacific nature of the rest of his doctrines. They were of far greater political importance than any religious argument between Jew and Jew and than the new interpretations which Jesus was placing upon the keeping of the Sabbath, the showing of mercy as opposed to strict justice, and other purely spiritual matters.

Inevitably the suspicions and enmity of the Roman authorities began to grow. They had seen too many disturbances caused by Jewish nationalists and in particular by the militant wing of the Jewish resistance movement—the Zealots. What was the true message which Jesus was preaching? Was it apparent pacifism or a scarcely veiled call for the establishment of a new kingdom? Was the first a mere cloak for the second? The Romans were political realists, analysing events in pragmatic terms and much more concerned with practical results than with theoretical intentions. Even if Jesus were sincere in teaching his followers to love their enemies, what was the likely outcome of his work as a whole? If the Jewish people were being continually exhorted to establish a new kingdom and to pray daily for its coming, then surely only unrest and violence could be the outcome.

He began to have enemies too among the scribes and chief priests of the Jewish religion, centred on the great Temple in Jerusalem. In many of his sermons he had not hesitated to attack the scribes and Pharisees and to exhort his listeners to seek a greater and truer piety than theirs. They saw him increasingly as a threat to their own authority and to the true following of the law. Jesus was clearly aware of this and went out of his way more than once to explain that he was not seeking to diminish the law by "one jot or one tittle" (Matthew 5:18). He denied categorically that he was impeding the law: "Think not that I am come to destroy the Law, or the prophets: I am not come to destroy, but to fulfil" (Matthew 5:17). The exact following of the law (the Torah) was, and remains to this day, the essence of Jewish piety. That Jesus found it necessary to declare specifically that his teachings were not directed to any abatement of that piety or as an encouragement to disregard the law indicates the suspicions that he had aroused among the Orthodox and the kind of things which chief priests and Temple authorities were angrily saying about him.

Each group realized that they could rely on support of other parties should the time come to discredit or to destroy the new teacher. There was no love lost between Pilate and King Herod (Luke 22:12). But it would have been apparent to Pilate that should Jesus in fact be making a bid for the kingdom of Judea, Herod's interests and the interests of the Roman power would be identical and he could confidently look to Herod for support. We have already seen the bloody cloud of anxiety that lowered over the heart and mind of old King Herod. Realising how tenuous were his rights to his kingdom, he feared every rival and did not hesitate to execute his own sons to protect his power. The younger Herod had shown no such extreme paranoia, but his case was much the same as that of his predecessor, and no doubt he was equally sensitive to any threat to his throne, particularly if it came from a man descended from the legendary house of David. Pilate must have known that he could exploit Herod's sense of insecurity and win his support for any move he might have to make against Jesus in the future. The murder of John was grim evidence for this view.

True, there was at present considerable hostility between Pilate and Herod, and matters could hardly be otherwise. In Pilate, Herod had a continual reminder of the illusory nature of his own powers, which were not merely supported but also limited by the will of the prefect. In Herod, Pilate had a source of constant irritation; because of the established policy of the central government in Rome and its representative in Syria, he could not rule his province with undiluted authority, as could most governors. He had to accept the nagging presence of local barbarian rulers, of whom Herod was one, and govern through them. This blurred the outlines of his personal power and forever involved him in native politics, a burden from which governors of other provinces were largely free. But political realities would outweigh personal irritation on both sides. He had only to stress to Herod those aspects of Jesus' teaching which referred to the coming of the new kingdom and so to demonstrate that Jesus, descended as he was from David and enjoying the support of multitudes of the people, represented a threat to his power far more perilous than that posed by the Baptist.

The Jewish religious authorities in their turn could exploit another political force—the party of the Zealots. Any open or formal alliance between the priesthood and the Zealots was unthinkable. Caiaphas had been appointed by the Romans. He had seen high priests come and go in bewildering succession at the whim of an earlier Roman governor. He knew that he depended utterly on Rome's goodwill for the security of his office. There could be no question whatever of forfeiting Rome's support by collaborating with the Zealot party, whose members were fanatically dedicated to the overthrow of Rome's authority by force of arms. But Caiaphas and, to a lesser extent, his colleagues could foresee circumstances in which they could exploit the Zealot party's popular following to belittle Jesus. They had only to show him as one whose pacifism was greater than his patriotism and who was prepared passively to accept Rome's alien rule. Such a move would be grotesquely dishonest, since such a policy of traitorous appeasement was in fact that of Caiaphas. But in politics success does not always lie with the honest, nor is it always denied to the cynical and cunning.

To achieve their purpose, the priesthood had merely to emphasise the pacific aspect of Jesus' teaching and to challenge him as to whether or not he supported the Roman power and whether he included the tyrannous officials and swaggering soldiers among the enemies whom he was exhorting his followers to love. If it could be shown that Jesus was preaching such a doctrine, then those of his followers who sympathised with the Zealot movement would fall away from him and could be counted on to support any plans to discredit or destroy him.

The priests could collect a great deal of evidence to further their arguments in this direction. Apart from the general exhortations to accept persecution, to love one's enemies, and to submit peacefully to violence, there was also the notorious fact that Jesus had used his healing powers to cure the servant of a Roman centurion—an act hardly likely to endear him to the Zealot party (Matthew 8:5–13). True, the centurion was a friend of the Jewish people and had built a synagogue (Luke 7:5). But to the extremists he was nonetheless a member of the occupying forces and one of the instruments of the tyranny of Rome.

A direct confrontation between Jesus and his enemies became increasingly inevitable. It was precipitated when Jesus appeared to make a direct and public bid for the temporal throne of Judea and when his repeated parable of the kingdom seemed to take (from the point of view of both Pilate and Herod) a more sinister and menacing significance. Apparently a claimant to earthly power, he seemed to emerge clearly as a political enemy of the state.

# 12

# Palm Sunday

We have already seen how emperors of the later Roman Empire made an official and ceremonial procession into the city of Rome and how this became an important ceremonial occasion, known as the *Adventus*, or Arrival. The last days of Jesus on earth opened with an event very like the entry of an emperor into his capital city and would have been seen by his contemporaries, Roman and Jewish alike, as neither more nor less than an *Adventus*—the entry of an earthly ruler into his capital.

The feast of the Passover is one of the great climaxes of the Jewish religious year. It commemorated the time when the descendants of Israel, who had for generations been held as bondsmen in Egypt, made their way under the leadership of Moses from the oppression of

Pharaoh to the freedom of Canaan—the land which their God had promised them. More especially, it commemorated the dramatic evidence which their God had then given of his especial relationship with his chosen people. To compel the Pharaoh to let the children of Israel go free, God had caused the Angel of Death to stalk grimly among the towns and villages of Egypt, taking away all the firstborn of the land into his grisly keeping. But the angel had passed over the dwelling places of the Jews. That he might do so, their houses had to be clearly distinguishable. So God had ordered the Jews to smear their doorposts with the blood of sacrificial lambs. Before they embarked on their long and hazardous journey across the Sinai Desert, they feasted on the flesh of these lambs, drank a cup of wine, and made a festival of what would be their last civilised meal for many a weary week, for they had a wide desert to cross and the perils of Pharaoh's pursuit to contend with. They departed when the moon was full, so that they could make haste by night before the forces of Pharaoh were aware of their escape. Thereafter the feast was annually remembered, and the festival is held to this day.

Many themes run through the Passover feast. First, it is a time of gladness and thanksgiving to God for the favours and mercy he extended to his people. Second, it renews the idea of sacrifice and the doctrine of the scapegoat. The lambs whose flesh had been eaten with bitter herbs at the last supper which the Jews were to eat before the flight to freedom had, by their meek and uncomplaining deaths, saved the people from the Angel of Death, taking upon themselves, by their meekness and gentleness, the sorrows and sins of all the people. The meat was thus not merely the garnishing of a gay feast, but the flesh of the sacrifice and a commemoration of God's mercy.

Because of the supreme importance of this festival, it was customary for all Jews who could make the journey to come into Jerusalem. They thronged from all the towns and villages of Judea to celebrate the Passover in the national capital and to worship in the Temple, which stood on the same site as that built by the great King Solomon. Jesus, like any other Jew of his time, was resolved to go to Jerusalem for the Passover feast. We know, from the story of his preaching in the Temple as a boy, that his parents were accustomed to take him thither. For him therefore it was an annual and accustomed pilgrimage.

But on this his last visit he entered the city, not as a pilgrim but as a king. And he did this with great deliberation, accepting and even seeming to seek all the symbols of regality. This entry into Jerusalem on the Sunday before the Passover feast was the true *Adventus* of Jesus as king of Israel.

Before passing through the city gates, he sent two of his disciples to bring a young ass on which he might ride into the capital, thus showing a deliberate intention to make a ceremonial entry. Next, he made no demur when people cast their clothing before him so that his mount might ride into the city over a carpet of gay garments. He was too learned in the Scriptures not to be aware of the royal significance of these actions, for it was written: "They hasted, and took every man his garment, and put it under him on the top of the stairs, and blew with trumpets, saying, Jehu is king" (II Kings 9:13). Nor is there any record of his having declined the royal acclamation which the crowd offered him. They gave him the high greeting of "Hosanna." They hailed him openly as the son of David (Matthew 21:9). They called blessings on him as a king (Luke 19:38). When he was asked by some of the Pharisees to rebuke his disciples for this royal greeting, he answered proudly: "I tell you that, if these should hold their peace, the stones would immediately cry out" (Luke 19:40). Specially they greeted him as "the king of Israel, that cometh in the name of the Lord" (John 12:13). They cast palm branches before him, bestrewing his path as they would bestrew the road before a king.

Here, for Roman eyes, was no longer the mild and pacific teacher of tolerance and submission, with one topic on which they might have doubts, that of the kingdom. Here was a man entering the capital city of the province quite clearly as a king, accepting the cheers of the people as of right and apparently making a serious bid for the kingship of Judea. This was not religious leadership but political meddling that came dangerously near to sedition.

Pilate, with his past experience of Jewish religious fervour, could not but be alarmed. It was already known that Jesus had gained an enormous following as a religious teacher. Would he receive the same massive support as an open claimant to the throne? If so, how could bloodshed and armed rebellion possibly be avoided? Jerusalem was always overcrowded at the feast of the Passover, with visitors pouring in from all over the country. A crowded city is always a dangerous city from any government's point of view, and Rome normally brought in extra troops during this time. The extraordinary entry of Jesus would have added both to the excitement of the people and to the apprehensions of the garrison commander.

Jesus had already won the enmity of Caiaphas, the high priest, and of his colleagues. They hated him not merely as a disturber of the old ways of their religion but as one who might endanger their own political position with the Romans. If they were to let him flourish unchallenged, his following would increase beyond all bounds. He would become not merely a religious but a political menace. "And the Romans shall come and take away both our place and nation" (John 11:48).

Caiaphas rebuked those of his colleagues who gave voice to these fears, pointing out that the solution lay within their own power. They had failed to consider "that it is expedient for us that one man should die for the people, and that the whole nation perish not" (John 11:49–50).

Perhaps the imminence of the Passover prompted Caiaphas to express himself in that particular manner. Just as the slaughter of the lambs in Egypt had caused the Angel of Death to pass over the nation of the Jews, so the destruction of Jesus might cause Rome's wrath to pass over the same nation today. Caiaphas' words were more than a grim foreboding of his own quite cynical intention; they were an explicit expression of the role which he intended Jesus to play as the sacrificial lamb. We do not know what specific fear prompted Caiaphas to suggest the destruction of Jesus in order to placate the Roman power. It was perhaps a generalised fear that Jesus was a troublemaker and that should trouble arise, then the Jewish people could only be the losers. More selfishly, he himself might well be ousted from his high office as one who had failed to keep the peace. If he were to succeed in seizing and destroying Jesus, it had to be with the full knowledge of the Roman power. Later events suggest that he had already begun to conspire with at least some of the Roman officials.

Certainly the triumphal and regal entry of Jesus into Jerusalem must have begun to arouse among the Romans apprehension of troubles to come. The manner of his entry made him an inevitable focus for the Zealots and their supporters. The crowd who hailed him as a king were not the same as those who had followed him as a healer and religious teacher. Among them in that crowded city there were undoubtedly Zealots and sympathisers of the Zealots who saw Jesus as the nation's best hope. If a descendant of David was now openly resolved to reestablish the kingdom, then no power on earth could this time prevent them from sweeping the Romans out of their beloved land. Once more they would receive their land from the hand of God, and the glory of the Davidic kingdom would be bloodily restored. Late into the night there must have been excited and secret talk of how the people of Israel would once more drive their enemies before them like leaves before the wind, as they had done in the reign of King Saul and in the days of the boy David.

Because of the Passover feast the authorities were already on the alert. Pilate himself was in the city, and, as usual, the garrison had been increased to provide an adequate number of troops to police the unquiet city. For the Romans, if trouble was to come, they were ready. For the Jewish patriots—moderates and Zealots alike—the occasion was one of great promise. A leader had declared himself, had accepted their patriotic plaudits. The restoration of the kingdom was near.

For Caiaphas and his colleagues Palm Sunday represented an insolent threat to their own and their nation's security under Rome. It hardened their resolve to sacrifice one man's life for the good of the people at large. We know that there had already been a violent episode. The records tell us that a man named Barabbas had at about this time been convicted of sedition and murder and was to be put to death by crucifixion (Mark 15:7). Caiaphas wanted no repetition of this, no further insult or provocation offered to the Roman power.

For Herod, who was also in Jerusalem, Palm Sunday was somewhat a wry jest. How could a humble religious teacher, the son of an artisan, however high his descent and however royal his lineage, make any serious bid for the throne? The strange man mounted on the ass, although the people had royally proclaimed him, was more a matter for mockery than fear, and bitter was the mockery to which Herod would shortly subject him.

Many men made many different judgements on the advent of this new king of Israel. Out of those judgements sprang many decisions as to what action should be taken. Political, nationalistic, religious, and imperial forces all began to operate and to create new and unlikely regroupings of power—all converging on the figure of Jesus.

In the event, the Zealots and their sympathisers were

to be disappointed, and out of their disillusion, fear and cruelty were alike to grow. Caiaphas' plan was to be put into action, and in it both the Roman prefect and Herod the Tetrarch were to be compelled to participate. And the new king, so recently and so royally greeted, was to die. But during the days immediately preceding the Passover feast it began to appear that the hope of the patriots would be realised, for Jesus, during those last days in Jerusalem, had seemed to be acting with more authority and positivism than he had before shown. He attacked the scribes and Pharisees vehemently and outspokenly, berating them as fools. As leaders they were blind and in their actions they were hypocrites. These were the descendants of the men of old who had slaughtered the prophets of God (Matthew 24).

He then made an open and violent challenge to the authorities of the Temple. Within the precincts there crowded traders, selling doves and oxen to the worshippers so that they might make the proper sacrifices. There were also the money changers, ready for a profit to exchange the Roman coinage, so that the devout could pay their temple dues. These money changers sat at their tables in one of the outer courtyards, plying their trade alongside the sellers of the sacrificial doves and oxen. The practice was sanctified by long usage and was entirely acceptable to the Temple authorities. But Jesus stormed into the courtyard, having first made himself a whip out of small cord (John 2:15). He blazed with more than mortal anger, overturned the tables of the money changers so that the precious coins lay scattered on the paving stones of the courtyard, and violently drove out the traders.

Many of the crowds now thronging the city and the Temple had not encountered Jesus before. Some had seen him for the first time when he entered the city as king. They had heard him rebuking the scribes and Pharisees and now saw him exercising such authority as only a king might dare display. All these actions of Jesus would have provided encouragement to the militants and their supporters. Here at last was a man to lead them, a man without fear and one who did not hesitate to use force in the very precincts of the Temple to purify religious practices and to reform ancient abuses. Here was the king they had awaited. Here was the king they could follow, sword in hand, to a final victory against the hated foreign oppressors and the sycophantic priesthood.

The cries of "Hosanna" still echoed in men's hearts. How was it that within such a few days the cries had changed to an insistent clamour of "Crucify him! Crucify him!"

First, the priesthood now actively sought to reveal Jesus either as one who defied Rome's authority or as a traitor to the national cause. So it was now that the chief priests planted a man in the crowd to ask Jesus the trick question about whether or not it was legitimate for a pious Jew to pay taxes to the occupying power. But Jesus was not to be drawn. He called for someone in the crowd to hand him a coin and pointed out that it bore Caesar's portrait. He told his listeners that it was quite proper to give back to Caesar money that was clearly already his. The answer was as astute as the question was politically loaded. Neither the Roman authorities nor the patriots could take offence. So the priests failed to alienate Jesus from those of his followers who sympathised with the Zealots, and equally they had failed in their alternative plan of persuading the Roman authorities that he was preaching open sedition.

Still pursuing this new and more authoritative policy, Jesus foretold the total destruction of the city and Temple (Matthew 24:2; Mark 13:3). This was a statement quite intolerable to the Temple authorities. Jesus, it seemed, was adopting the methods of the prophets of ancient times who, purporting to tell future events, were in fact rebuking those set in authority over the people. Their dreadful warnings of disaster were no more than arrogant threats of divine retribution unless their own advice was followed.

The Temple authorities, in the persons of Caiaphas and most of his colleagues, finally concluded that the time had come to destroy this vehement and increasingly outspoken troublemaker. They had two problems. The first was to arrest him privily when he was alone. Such was his following in the city that to seize him openly would be to precipitate disturbances and even full-scale riots. Their second problem was to decide on some charge which lay within the jurisdiction of their council, the Sanhedrin.

Their solution to the first problem was to find one of Jesus' disciples to assist them in making an arrest in secret. They selected Judas Iscariot. They also decided that the charge that they would bring against him would not be political (since for that they would require the open support of the Roman authorities) but religious. Surely they could charge him with blasphemy, both for the unorthodoxy of his teaching and also for the cures he had effected and the doctrines he had taught, since he did all these things in his own name rather than, in the manner of the ancient prophets, in the name of God.

What motives prompted Judas to play such an appalling part in the arrest and death of his friend and teacher? Perhaps the answer lay in the area of politics. There had been three national heroes who had borne the name of Judas.

A century and a half before the birth of Jesus there had been the great Judas, son of the priest Mattathias, who had delivered the Jewish people from their Syrian conquerors. In battle after battle he had defeated the finest armies and the greatest generals whom the Syrians could send against him. He earned immortal glory and the proud name of Maccabaeus—the Hammer—whose strokes had so shattered the enemies of Israel. His fame was legendary:

> So he gat his people great honour and put on a breastplate as a giant, and girt his warlike harness about him, and he made battles, protecting the host with his sword. In his acts he was like a lion, and like a lion's whelp roaring for his prey (Apocrypha, I Maccabees 3:3–4).

More recently, when the ageing King Herod had affronted all religous Jews by erecting a great golden eagle above the gateway of the Temple, it was a man named Judas who with others tore down the offending image. Judas, with about forty of his adherents, was taken prisoner and brought before King Herod, whom he heroically defied. He and the others were burned at the stake. That same night the moon suffered an eclipse, as if symbolising the sorrow of the people.[1]

Finally, there had been Judas of Galilee, who had led an armed rising against the Roman power when Jesus was a boy. His war of independence came very close to success. The governor of Syria had been compelled to march his legions southwards to the rescue of the hard-pressed garrison of Judea. Only then were Judas and his followers crushed, and many hundreds were publicly crucified. Jesus as a child may have seen scores of hideous crosses bearing the tormented bodies of the defeated Zealots.

Judas Iscariot's name strongly suggests that his family were ardent patriots and had named him after those national heroes. Had he followed Jesus knowing that the latter, as a descendant of the house of David, could provide the very leadership which a new and successful uprising against the Romans would require? Had he, like so many others of Jesus' listeners, misunderstood the continual references to "the kingdom"? Was his heart filled with martial hopes that a new leader had arisen to "put on a breastplate as a giant, and girt his warlike harness about him"? Certainly he would have been very conscious of the name he bore and the national heroes that name commemorated.

So perhaps Judas was prompted by the same motives which so swiftly changed the adulation of the multitudes in Jerusalem into bitter hatred, transforming the cries of "Hosanna" into a clamour for crucifixion.

During his last days in Jerusalem, Jesus made one simple and categorical statement which must have done more to alienate him from the Zealots and their supporters than all the cunning traps which his enemies had tried to set for him. When he was being examined by Pilate, he said, "My kingdom is not of this world" (John 19:36).

No doubt the issue had been discussed earlier with his disciples. If Judas had become aware of Jesus' final renunciation of any temporal kingdom, then his hopes, which had been so high on Palm Sunday, would have been totally dashed. He had to face the bitter knowledge that he, a militant patriot, had wasted two years of his life in following a master who had no intention of leading any armed attack either against the Roman authorities or their puppet rulers. Anger is the frequent fruit of disillusionment. No lifelong enemy is more hostile than a onetime friend who suddenly realises that the friendship has been based on illusion and that his friend has defeated his hopes and frustrated all his deepest longings.

The scene was now set for the final drama.

But before this took place, Jesus and his followers were to celebrate Passover. They were to sit down together for the roast lamb, the cup of wine, and the unleavened bread that formed the traditional repast.

Jesus, aware of the complex plots that were being made against him, saw the sorrowful relevance of the feast to his own case, as well as its irony, more bitter than the herbs with which the meat was dressed. He would eat the flesh of the lamb, the sacrificial animal whose death had saved the people of Israel centuries ago. But, aware of the intentions of Caiaphas, he knew that he too would shortly be sacrificed for what the high priest considered to be the safety of the nation. He and the paschal dish were one; the lamb's flesh was his flesh, and the wine of the feast was the blood he would be required to offer as the slaughtered sacrifice—not merely of his own people but, as he now knew it to be, of all the nations of the world.

# 13

# The Feast and the Arrest

It was becoming increasingly clear to all the disciples that the Pharisees and the priests were resolved to take Jesus and destroy him. John reports (7:30, 32) that they had already sought to arrest him on an earlier occasion. Also they had previously tried to trap him into persuading his followers to break the holy law. Certain scribes and Pharisees had once brought to him a woman who had been taken in the act of adultery. They reminded him that the law of Moses ordained that such a woman should suffer death by stoning and asked him what he proposed. If he had suggested forgiveness, then he would have been shown up as an irresponsible teacher who was advocating a breach in the immutable laws which Moses had delivered directly from God. On the other hand, had he ordered the crowd to stone the woman, then all his earlier preaching of compassion and forgiveness would have seemed mere hypocrisy. But his reply gave neither alternative. By calling on those without sin to begin the ritual execution by stoning, he was loyal to the law of Moses. But he knew that shame and conscience would prevent any man from throwing the first stone. The woman was saved and the plot of the scribes and Pharisees frustrated (John 18:2–9).

Now, during those last days in Jerusalem, the priests made a more direct and open challenge. As he was walking in the Temple, the chief priests and the scribes, together with the elders of the Temple, asked him by whose authority he taught and had performed his miracles and cures. Again a trap was being laid. Had he claimed that he was working under God's authority, then a charge of blasphemy might well be successful. But had he claimed that he was doing all things in his own name, then the charge of blasphemy would have been even surer of success. Again his answer avoided the anticipated alternatives. Remembering how the Temple authorities had neglected the teachings of John the Baptist, he met their questions with a counterquestion. Was the baptism which John had given to the people based on a heavenly authority, or did it come from mortal men? The questioners realised that they in turn had been trapped. If they said that John's authority was from God, then how could they answer for having neglected him, for failing to support him, and for allowing him to be executed? Had they said that the authority was merely from men, how could they account for the fact that John by now was generally accepted as a prophet? Abashed, they answered that they could not tell. Jesus, having thus reversed the roles of questioner and questioned, replied that neither could he tell them by what authority he himself had embarked on his mission (Mark 11:27–33; Matthew 21:23–27; Luke 20:1–8).

But he was not content merely to defeat the challenges of the priesthood by brilliant dialectic. The time had come for the revelation of his authority. He openly declared himself as coming from God: "I am not come of myself, but He that sent me is true, Whom ye know not, but I know Him: for I am from Him and He hath sent me" (John 7:28–29).

From all these exchanges two things were now manifestly clear. First, Jesus himself knew that his life was in danger and that the Temple authorities, however careful and measured were his answers to their questions, were resolved to arrest and destroy him. Second, it became increasingly apparent to Judas that Jesus was a religious and not a political leader. Here was no martial king of a revived Davidic kingdom. Here was no armed and armoured captain of the Jewish people. The teachings of forgiveness to one's enemies and patience under persecution were after all no mere covers for an underlying intention to lead the people towards a new and triumphant kingdom. They were just what they had always purported to be—parables and metaphors to convey a purely spiritual message.

Because both Jesus and Judas, like all the others of his followers, were Orthodox Jews, the knowledge that had come to them could not cause them to brush aside the sacred festival of the Passover. Both had to play their parts within the framework of that festival. By now Jesus knew that it was the last occasion when he would eat the lamb and drink the wine, and Judas knew that immediately thereafter he would assist in the arrest of his onetime leader, so as to destroy the man who had failed to fulfil both the prophecies and his own dreams of the reestablishment of the visible kingdom.

Before the feast Judas went to the chief priests and the captains of the Temple guard. He promised to help them to arrest Jesus quietly, away from any crowd, thereby avoiding the risk of disturbances. They undertook to pay him for the service, as authorities the world over have always paid their informers and as they continue to do to this day (Luke 22:1–6). Now that Caiaphas had made sure that he could arrest Jesus secretly, he was able to inform those Roman officials whom he had made privy to his plot. It was no doubt now that he arranged for a detachment of Roman troops to accompany the Temple guard when the time came for the arrest. Judas himself was unaware of this. Only later was he to learn that his action in assisting in Jesus' arrest would be used to the advantage of the hated Roman occupying power.

Jesus was aware of what Judas had done. He knew Judas well, and there can be little doubt that Judas, before taking the final and awesome step, had expostulated with Jesus and told him of the bitterness of his disappointment. The entry into Jerusalem, which had seemed to be Jesus' declaration of kingship and the prelude to throwing out the Romans by force of arms (as Judas Maccabaeus had hurled out the Syrians), had proved to be a wretched anticlimax in Judas' eyes. Jesus would have had to face an angry, argumentative Judas and realised that there could be but one outcome. But this did not deter him from arranging to celebrate the feast of the Passover. Before the feast he told his disciples in clear terms that he would be betrayed and executed (Matthew 26:2).

He then instructed Peter and John to prepare for the feast in secret, so that his arrest might not prevent this last ceremonial. He had already made arrangements with someone in the city who was willing to place his house at the disposal of Jesus and his followers—not without some danger to himself from the authorities. Jesus told Peter and John to go into the city where their host would be carrying a pitcher of water, by which sign they would recognise him (Luke 22:9, 10). The man led them into an upper room where supper was already laid. Jesus followed with the rest of the apostles and presided over the feast.

Knowing what he knew of the plans of Caiaphas, he now clearly identified himself with the sacrificial lamb. It was this explicit identification, made when—in accordance with usual custom—he blessed the bread and wine of the feast, which was to form the central theme of all later Christian worship, the ceremony of the Communion. Christians are divided as to whether his identification was and is a metaphorical or a physical one.

Perhaps this division is less important than the protagonists of either view believe. It is perhaps enough for us to see in Jesus' words and actions at that supper his certain knowledge of his coming death and his realisation that by the shedding of his blood he was creating a new Passover. Caiaphas would have his will; the death of one man would save the nation; the Zealot party would no longer make him a focus for a new and violent uprising; if his teaching had been of any avail and if his disciples proved to be true branches of the vine which he had planted, then his death would save his people not only from political and military danger; it would save them—and perhaps all the nations of the world—from the sad bequest of sin which they had inherited from their first ancestor, Adam the disobedient.

After the blessing and during the supper Jesus privately disclosed to those who sat next to him that he knew of Judas' intention. Mark (14:18–21) and Matthew (26:21–25) both report that he then told all at supper that one of them would betray him. Perhaps this came as no surprise to Judas if, before the festival, there had been those long and angry discussions of which we have spoken. But what followed after Jesus' private conversation with those nearest to him must have come as a great shock to Judas. The disciples had looked at one another in fear and doubt, and one of them asked which of them would play the traitor's part. Jesus replied that it was the man to whom he would give a sop of bread from the dish, and forthwith gave the sop to Judas. He then said to Judas, so that all could hear him, "That thou doest, do quickly" (Mark 13:27).

The other disciples had no inkling of the inner meaning of those words. Since Judas was the treasurer of the party, they thought that Jesus was sending him out on some errand or other to buy further necessaries for the feast.

But Judas knew. He knew not only that Jesus was aware of the plans but that he acquiesced in them. Jesus was telling him that he would go willingly to the slaughter like the paschal lamb with which he had so clearly identified himself. Judas hurried out, and after he had left, Jesus began to make his farewell to his friends. They protested their loyalty and vied with one another as to who should prove his greatest supporter in the coming adversity. But Jesus told them that his leadership was not like that of the pagan kings, under whom those who exercised the greatest authority were considered the greatest men. In the invisible kingdom to which he was calling them the greatest should be accounted the most junior, and the chief among them should be considered as the servant (Luke 22:25–26).

Jesus now told his disciples that where once he had sent them on their journeys barefoot and with neither purse nor luggage, they should now go out on their new journey complete with purse and a bag for their belongings. The words that followed were startling. Had Judas still been there, they might have prompted him to think that he had entirely misjudged his leader. He said, "He that hath no sword, let him sell his garment and buy one" (Luke 22:36).

He was told that they had two swords among them, and he said that this was enough. What was this sudden reference to weapons of war? Why was he, who was prepared to go unresistingly to his own death, enjoining his friends to carry arms? If Judas had still been present, might he not even at that eleventh hour have changed his mind? Was Jesus after all about to lead his people in arms against the national enemy? But Judas, hurrying through the night to the Temple authorities, was now committed to the dreadful task he had undertaken.

The feast over, Jesus went across the small brook of Cedron into the public Garden of Gethsemane. Two years before on the Mount of Temptation he had made the momentous decision not to follow his destiny as a prince of the house of David or to lay claim to a temporal kingdom, but to dedicate his life to religious teaching. So now in the Garden of Gethsemane the same decision, with more immediate agony, had to be renewed. Escape was still possible, although time was short. The Garden of Gethsemane was well known to Judas. But Jesus had only to go into hiding to some place where Judas coud not lead the Temple guards to find him. The rest of his disciples were loyal and resolute. Peter was carrying one of the swords.

The Passover moon was shining over the sleeping city. It would have been a dangerous but not impossible adventure for him and his companions to leave the garden and make their way to some suitable hiding place. They could have evaded or indeed have fought against any Roman police patrols.

The temptation to do so was immense. Otherwise he faced death in one of two ways, both hideous. If convicted of blasphemy by the Temple authorities, then he would die by the ritual cruelty of stoning. Death would come to him tardily, after he had been slowly battered into unconsciousness, to die in a pool of his own blood.

But the high priest might well hand him over to the Roman power so as to derive the maximum political advantage from his death by demonstrating his total loyalty. In that circumstance he would meet his end by crucifixion, and on the cross men died of no mortal and final wound but of slow pain which so continued until human flesh could no longer bear it and retreated into the stillness of death.

The choice made, at the cost of so much suffering on the Mount of Temptation, had as its outcome this further and even more bitter choice. It was one thing on the Mount of Temptation to renounce that earthly kingdom which was his right by blood and to follow the example of his kinsman John, calling his people to a revival and purification of their ancient faith. It was another thing to make an urgent choice between death by torment and a desperate dash to safety and obscurity.

The choice had in fact already been made. Had he not taught his people to pray that God's will might be done? If, as it seemed, it was God's will that he should be the sacrifice of a new Passover, then how could he fail to follow his own teaching? Alone, with his friends a stone's throw away, he prayed in the terms of the prayer he had taught. Desperately he wanted not to drink the cup of pain that was being prepared for him, but he could ask for this only if it were God's will. "Father, if Thou be willing, remove this cup from me: nevertheless not my will, but Thine, be done" (Luke 22:42). He underwent a far greater degree of suffering than during his first temptation. "And being in an agony he prayed more earnestly: and his sweat as it were great drops of blood falling down to the ground" (Luke 22:44).

Sure of his own steadfastness, he still had some lingering doubts about the resolution of his companions, whose love for him might well outrun what he conceived to be their duty—namely, to stand meekly aside while their friend was taken to certain death. He exhorted them to pray also, "Lest ye enter into temptation" (Luke 22:46).

Immediately afterwards a group of Temple guards, accompanied by Judas, entered the garden. With them was a detachment of Roman troops. The priests who had sent out the patrol were taking no chances. If Judas failed to lead them to Jesus in a private place and if they were compelled to arrest him in the crowded city, they might have to face an angry mob. So the squad was not a small one. They were armed with swords and truncheons, fully prepared for any riot that might ensue, and carried lanterns and torches. They saw the twelve shadowy figures of Jesus and his apostles dimly in the moonlit gardens. But they could not be sure which of the men was their quarry. Judas quickly explained that he would identify Jesus with a kiss. He went up to Jesus, kissed him, and greeted him as Master.

Contemptuously rejecting the secret betrayal, Jesus challenged the guard and asked them whom they were seeking to arrest. When they told him, as he expected, that it was Jesus of Nazareth, he proudly said, "I am he." Then, with a touch of that imperious anger which we have seen during those last days in Jerusalem, he, the prisoner, gave orders to those who had arrested him, commanding them to let his friends go (John 18:1–11). They recognised the authority with which he spoke, and the disciples were allowed to depart.

But before this, one of them offered violent and desperate resistance to the guard. The impetuous Peter took his sword and attacked one of the soldiers, wounding him in the ear. Jesus healed the wound and reprimanded Peter.

Still defiant, Jesus rebuked his captors for having come armed against him and for having arrested him secretly by night. He was no wrongdoer, no fugitive. Proudly he said, "Are ye come out, as against a thief, with swords and staves to take me?" He reminded them that he had openly preached in the Temple every day since his entry into the city. Why had they not arrested him there? (Mark 14:48, 49). These were words which might have been used by a proud king against rebellious soldiers, or they might have been the words of one conscious of divine authority, who had no cause—despite his earlier agony of choice—to fear any man.

So the guards, no doubt bewildered by the regal (or was it divine?) bearing of their prisoner, led him away in the moonlight to the house of Annas, a former high priest.

# 14

# The Three Trials

The Romans had made of their empire a single political unity. From the Danube to the Atlantic and from Hadrian's Wall in Britain to the Mediterranean coast of Africa, the diverse nations acknowledged the Eternal City as the seat of the civilised world's central government. Rome maintained the unity of these many lands through two instruments.

First there was the army. But even at the height of her power she rarely had more than a quarter of a million men under arms. This was a small force with which to police such a vast area, to guard the perilous frontiers, to wage almost constant war along the turbulent borderlands between her dominions and those of the Persian Empire.

But more important than the glittering armour and

burnished weapons of her army was her second instrument of unity—the law. Rome introduced her courts and legislation throughout her dominions. Roman justice and Roman law were among the strongest bonds which bound together the many people of her empire. All young men of noble birth in Rome underwent a long course of training, holding first junior and then senior magistracies, as well as military appointments. It was such men who governed the provinces, bringing to them the efficiency and justice of Rome.

There was an elegance and precision about Roman law that remained the envy of succeeding generations. To this day it forms the basis of the legal codes of many nations.

The punishments they inflicted were cruel, but the legal processes by which a man was judged were on the whole fair and reasonable. The humblest Roman citizen (as the career of Paul was later to demonstrate) had the right of appeal to the emperor himself. No Roman citizen could suffer the dreadful punishment of crucifixion.

But although Judea was a Roman province, Jesus was not a Roman citizen. He ranked as a *perigrinus,* the citizen of a conquered territory who had to acknowledge the final authority of Rome but who did not enjoy full civic rights.

Within such an orderly system how did it come about that he had to face three jurisdictions and undergo three separate trials?

The answer lies in the political lines of force that were at work in the province, at which we have already glanced. The Romans, always reluctant to interfere with the religious practices of their subject peoples, allowed the Jewish religious council (the Sanhedrin) to judge cases of religious law and to inflict their traditional punishments. The story of the woman taken in adultery illustrates this. She had been convicted by a local Jewish court within whose power it lay to impose the traditional sentence of death by stoning. Thus it was perfectly proper, in the context of the administrative organisation of the province, for Caiaphas and his colleagues to try Jesus—so long as the charge against him was that he was in breach of the religious law, the Torah.

Moreover, in provinces where Rome maintained native rulers, she allowed them to exercise jurisdiction over their own subjects. True, she held the ultimate authority in her own hands. But local cases could be tried by local rulers, and they had the power of life or death over their subjects. An example is old King Herod's slaughter of the children in Bethlehem, against which Rome made no protest. The execution of John the Baptist by Herod the Tetrarch provides another instance.

Finally Pilate, prefect of the province, could sit in judgement in all cases, applying the standard of Roman law and not the local customary law.

The three trials of Jesus precisely reflected this threefold situation. They also show how both Caiaphas and the tetrarch Herod were anxious to appease the Roman power and to use the trial of Jesus as a demonstration of their own loyalty, overriding their precise legal rights, to Caesar and his representatives.

So when on the night of his arrest Jesus was taken to

the house of Annas, there began the first of his three trials. Of all his disciples only Peter followed him as he was hustled by the guards and thrust into the house. But even Peter lacked the courage to do more than loiter in the servants' quarters, warming himself by the fire. When challenged by one of the servants that he was one of Jesus' followes, Peter denied all knowledge of him and crept away from the house.

Jesus was led before Annas and his colleagues, still surrounded by soldiers of the Temple guard, as if he were some violent prisoner who was likely to make a dash for freedom. To fulfil their purpose the Temple authorities had to convict Jesus on two grounds. First, so that their jurisdiction should be unchallenged, the charge had to be on some religious issue. A verdict of guilty on, for example, a charge of blasphemy would entitle them to put this troublemaker to death. But they had a further objective, that of placating the Roman authorities, of gaining the latter's participation in the execution of Jesus, and demonstrating their loyalty to Rome in having uncovered a dangerous rebel. To do this they had to show that Jesus, apart from any religous offences, was projecting himself as the Messiah, the Anointed One, the rightful king of Israel.

This last was a political matter, over which they themselves had no right of jurisdiction. But if they could prove this point, they could refer the case to Pilate himself, for any claimant to the throne of Judea was in rebellion against Rome. The gratitude they would earn from Pilate would fulfil Caiaphas' earlier words, that it was right for one man to die for the good of the nation.

So Jesus, surrounded by the soldiers of the Temple

guard, stood in the lamplight silently before Annas. The latter began at once to probe the question of blasphemy. He asked Jesus about his disciples and ordered him to give some account of his doctrines. Jesus answered disdainfully that he had been teaching openly in the synagogues and in the Temple and had never kept any of his teachings secret. He challenged Annas to produce witnesses from among those who had heard his preaching, adding, "They know what I said." One of the officers of the guard struck Jesus for this flash of insolence and asked him how he dared speak to Annas so. Jesus challenged the captain to make a formal statement if he knew of any evil thing which Jesus had ever taught. Annas did not pursue his interrogation but forthwith sent Jesus (as no doubt it was all along planned to do) to his son-in-law, Caiaphas, the high priest (John 17:19–24).

Everything had been made ready for the trial and an immediate conviction. Caiaphas had already assembled the Sanhedrin, consisting of all the chief priests together with the elders of the Temple and the scribes. Witnesses had been assembled and their stories rehearsed. But by the time Jesus was brought before Caiaphas it was found that none of the witnesses could agree together or plausibly support the charges. However, two men were found who were prepared to give evidence against the prisoner (Matthew 26:59–60; Mark 14:56–57). According to Luke (22:64), the guards had by now blindfolded Jesus. They played a grim blindman's buff with him, beating him and challenging him to use his prophetic powers to identify those who had struck him. Caiaphas, like Annas, began by pressing the charge of blasphemy. One of the two witnesses said that he had heard Jesus threaten to destroy the Temple (Matthew 26:61; Mark 14:58). Jesus made no answer and remained silent even when Caiaphas formally rose from his seat and demanded a reply.

Quite clearly the implication of the evidence was ridiculous. To condemn a man for blasphemy on the pretext that he had threatened to destroy a massive and enduring building was not to be considered. They could not plausibly put a man to death on such an outrageous pretext.

So Caiaphas moved swiftly to the second part of his plan—to prove Jesus to be a claimant to the throne of Judea. He still combined this with the charge of blasphemy by asking Jesus whether he was the Anointed One and whether he was also the Son of the Blessed. Was he the Messiah both in the political sense—an aspirant to the throne of Judea—and in the spiritual sense—in terms of the prophecy of Isaiah, one who claimed to be the Son of God himself? An affirmative reply to either part of the question would have been sufficient for Caiaphas' purpose. A confession that he was a claimant to the throne would have justified Caiaphas in referring him to the Roman authorities. An admission that he claimed to be the Son of God would equally have entitled the Sanhedrin to send their prisoner to Pilate, for there was only one son of a god on the mortal earth, and that was Tiberius Caesar himself. Moreover, it would have brought the case back within the scope of the Sanhedrin's religious jurisdiction. Would Jesus maintain the same unshakeable silence with which he had met the earlier questions? To the surprise and delight of Caiaphas and his colleagues, Jesus answered the question simply, positively, and briefly. He said, "I am . . . " (Mark 14:62).

Luke gives a slightly different account. When Caiaphas categorically asked Jesus whether he was the Anointed One, Luke reports Jesus as having broken his silence but nevertheless refusing to answer the question. "If I tell you," he said, "ye will not believe: and if I also ask you, you will not answer me nor let me go" (Luke 22:67–68). Perhaps this bitter reply, which made it clear to all that Jesus knew that he would find no justice at the Sanhedrin's hands but only a prearranged conviction, was made before the simple and proud "I am . . . " reported by Mark.

Caiaphas was jubilant. He tore his clothes in a gesture of ritual sorrow at finding himself in the presence of such high blasphemy. But it was in fact a gesture of triumph. Now they had Jesus safely convicted. And they had him on both grounds—as claimant to the throne and as a blasphemer. There was no need for further witnesses or for continuing the mockery of a trial. Caiaphas formally turned to his colleagues and asked for their verdict. They found him guilty and deserving of death.

The long night that had begun with Jesus taking the Passover supper among his friends had still not drawn to its close. The Sanhedrin could not yet take their prisoner to the prefect, who would be sleeping peacefully, unaware of the part Caiaphas had arranged for him to play. The examination of Jesus over, the escorting guards and members of the council gave vent to their feelings of relief that they had secured a conviction by a further outburst of violence against Jesus, striking him and spitting on him.

Some at least of the council were sympathetic. They did not dare to make any protest, but sympathisers there must have been. The trial by the Sanhedrin was, after all, a private one with none of Jesus' disciples present. Unless some friendly member of the council had later told them what had happened, no account of the trial could have appeared in the Gospels. The evangelists' narratives are so detailed that they seem to be based on eyewitness reports. Perhaps Joseph of Arimathea or Nicodemus, both sympathisers of Jesus and both members of the Sanhedrin, later told the disciples about the examination before Caiaphas. The two of them would have watched helplessly while Jesus was reviled and beaten before being led away.

The morning drew on, and everything was now ready for Caiaphas to put the second part of his plot into operation: to take Jesus before Pilate, as a demonstration of his and his colleagues' loyalty to Rome, and directly to involve the prefect in the execution of the prisoner. Jesus was taken to Pilate very early in the morning. The priests and elders could not enter the Roman building, since they were forbidden by the law to go to any Gentile's house during the Passover feast. So Pilate made his first concession to them by himself coming out of the building and greeting them outside. From the first he wanted no part in the business. He told the chief priests to take Jesus back and judge him according to their own law. He knew that the Sanhedrin had jurisdiction in all religious matters, and he was anxious not to become personally implicated or to involve Rome's authorities in what was purely a local and religious issue. But the priests insisted that he should try the prisoner, saying that it was not lawful for them to inflict capital punishment (John 18:28–31).

Their reply was both specious and sinister—specious since they did possess the right to try their own people for religious offences, sinister because it showed that they were already intent on the prisoner's death and that the proposed trial before Pilate was to be a mere formality.

Pilate now made his second concession. Instead of insisting, as a stronger man might have done, that the case should go back to the Sanhedrin despite their protests, he yielded to their demands and listened to the accusations. Basically there were two charges against Jesus—the claim to be king of the Jews and the blasphemous claim to be the Son of the Most High—the Son of God. Pilate would have been bound to sentence Jesus to death if either charge could be proved. If Jesus was laying claim to the kingdom of Judea, then he was guilty of sedition against the Roman authorities and death was his due. If he was claiming to be the Son of God, *filius divi,* then he was setting himself up as an equal of the emperor. In that case he would be guilty of lese majesty and, absurd though the charge might have seemed when levelled against one so obscure, of conspiring to seize imperial power.

In conformity with their plans, the chief priests accordingly emphasised the political aspects of Jesus' alleged offences. They told Pilate (Luke 23:2) that they had found the prisoner subverting the nation, forbidding the people to pay their lawful taxes to Rome, and claiming to be the Anointed One—the king of the Jewish nation.

Pilate opened his interrogation by asking Jesus specifically whether he was the king of the Jews. There are two reports of his reply. Matthew, Mark, and Luke record his having answered Pilate with the words "You have said so." Linguistically this phrase was almost certainly an affirmative. There is no word for "yes" in either Greek or Latin—the language used in the earliest forms of the Gospels—and agreement had to be expressed by this kind of phrase. Another reply of Jesus shows beyond doubt that he saw himself as a king but had his own interpretation of the word, for he made a statement to Pilate which must have come as a shattering blow for those of his supporters of the Zealot cause: "My kingdom is not of this world" (John 18:36). Pilate, eager though he was, as always, to satisfy the demands of the Jewish religious authorities, could not on the evidence find Jesus guilty of the charge of laying claim to the throne. Clearly he recognised the validity of the statement "My kingdom is not of this world." His decision also meant that he recognised that the claim of Jesus to be *filius divi* was made in a context quite different from the usages of imperial Rome. Jesus was not putting himself forward as the equal of Caesar. He was indulging in an immoderate and ridiculous religious claim, typical of his nation but practically harmless.

But before pronouncing final judgement, Pilate sought another way out of his dilemma and an escape from the stark choice between appeasement and justice. Learning that Jesus was a Galilean, he pointed out that the prisoner therefore came under the jurisdiction of Herod. To send the prisoner to Herod for judgement seemed an excellent solution to the tiresome problems posed by the charges. If he, a Roman official, sentenced Jesus to death as the Sanhedrin was insisting, then Jesus, after his death, might come to be seen as a victim of Roman oppression and the focus for future sedition and rebellion. But if Herod, himself a Jew, were to sentence Jesus to death, no such political consequences would arise any more than had been the case of John the Baptist. So Pilate sent Jesus to Herod, who was in Jerusalem for the Passover (Luke 23:6, 7).

Caiaphas saw that Pilate was not falling into his trap. His carefully laid plot was being frustrated, and he would neither gain favour in Roman eyes by his arrest of Jesus nor implicate Rome in the latter's execution.

Herod was both flattered and delighted by Pilate's action in sending the prisoner to him. From that day forward he and Pilate, who had long been enemies, became friends (Luke 23:12).

But Herod did not take the charges against Jesus seriously, nor did he give him any serious trial. With grim and bitter mockery he was content to remove the danger of any legitimate claim which Jesus might have to be king. With heavy sarcasm he had the prisoner dressed in a rich and princely garment and sent him back to Pilate.

The latter was still reluctant to inflict the death penalty on one whom he had found to be a just man. Unable simply to discharge the prisoner because of his continued desire to appease the Jewish authorities, he reminded the Sanhedrin of a long-established custom whereby at the feast of the Passover it was customary for the Roman authorities to release any Jewish prisoner selected by the Temple authorities. He reminded the chief priests of this and proposed that Jesus should be chosen for release. But the chief priests, as well as the crowds who were gathered outside the building, clamoured for his crucifixion and demanded the release of another prisoner, Barabbas. Although the figure of Barabbas lies in the shadows, some tentative conclusions can be drawn about him. Almost certainly he was a Zealot, for he already lay under sentence of death, having been found guilty of a "certain sedition made in the city and for murder" (Luke 23:19). The conjunction of sedition and murder strongly suggests some subversive political activity in the course of which a man had been killed. It was a measure of Pilate's anxiety to release Jesus that he should have offered, in exchange for the latter's life, freedom to such a politically dangerous man as Barabbas.

Finally, the name Barabbas itself is suggestive. *Bar* is the Hebrew for "the son of" and *abba* is the familiar word for "father," so that the name means simply, "Father's son." When members of resistance movements are picked up by the police of an occupying power, it is not uncommon for them to withold their real name, so "Father's son" would have been as good a *nom de guerre* as any, particularly if the agents of the occupying power had no fluent knowledge of one's own language. The evidence of the name alone is too tenuous to be significant, but it fits into the general picture of Barabbas as a Zealot.

This is supported by the crowd's reaction to Pilate's suggestion. Jesus' final renunciation of a temporal kingdom must have come as a terrible anticlimax to those who, as recently as the previous Sunday, had hailed him as king and as the potential leader of an armed attack against the Roman power. Now at his trial he had proclaimed himself as one who claimed no earthly kingdom and who was not to be the captain of a desperate and resolute army. Better far that a passive religious preacher, the validity of whose doctrines had been questioned by the high priest himself, should die than that a proven hero of the resistance movement, such as Barabbas, should be sacrificed for him. If Pilate wished to invoke the Passover amnesty, then it must be for Barabbas! So the crowd insisted upon release for Barabbas and death for Jesus: "Crucify him, crucify him!" (Luke 23:21).

Even at this eleventh hour Pilate tried to avoid passing sentence of death. He repeated that he found Jesus not guilty. As a compromise he offered to have Jesus scourged and then released. But even this the crowd refused and insisted on his death.

By now Pilate was totally out of sympathy with the prisoner's accusers. He found their charges unjust and their clamour cruel. But his policy of appeasement prevented him from making a final stand for what he knew to be just, and he forbore from setting free a man whom he had twice declared guiltless. So rather than risk any further unrest among the excited people, he finally passed sentence of death.

But he could not refrain from deriding the Sanhedrin and their ridiculous charge that this religious teacher had aspired to the throne. It was more in mockery of the accusers than of Jesus himself that he allowed the soldiers to take Jesus inside the building and to dress him as a king. Over his shoulders was placed a scarlet robe. They gave him a reed for a sceptre and placed on his head a royal diadem—woven from cruel thorns. And the soldiers acclaimed him as king of the Jews. Then they stripped him of the purple of regality and led him away to his death.

John's account of the trial lends support to the suggestion that Caiaphas had plotted to implicate Pilate, for when Pilate was trying to avoid giving the death sentence, the crowd shouted that if he let this man go, he would prove himself no friend to Caesar (John 19:12). This was a serious threat, implying that if Pilate released Jesus, the Sanhedrin would report the matter either to the emperor direct or to the governor of Syria.

This no doubt had an effect on Pilate, who maintained his ironic and bitter attitude to the very end. When a criminal was crucified, a notice describing his crime was placed on the cross. In further mockery of the accusers, Pilate ordered the notice for the cross of Jesus to be inscribed in Latin, Greek, and Hebrew with the words "This is Jesus of Nazareth, king of the Jews." The Sanhedrin were not merely offended but alarmed by the jibe. It implied that they had accepted Jesus as their king and would put them in political peril. They therefore asked Pilate to alter the notice to read that this man had said that he was king of the Jews. But Pilate, in his bitterness, curtly brushed their suggestion aside. "What I have written, I have written."

So the prophecy of Caiaphas and the forebodings of Jesus at the Passover supper were alike fulfilled. Jesus, who for so long had taught mercy, the forgiveness of one's enemies, and love for all men, was executed as a criminal, himself finding no mercy. He died as he had lived, true to the immensely difficult doctrines he had preached. He called on God to forgive those who were so cruelly putting him to death, and his last words were from one of the poems written by his great ancestor, David. The blood of David had brought him no regal inheritance. It had placed him and his parents in mortal peril when he was a baby, and it had finally brought him to a most hideous death.

A strange echo of the trial before Pilate is to be found in the works of Josephus. Describing the outbreak of the war between the Romans and Jews in A.D. 70, he records that "Jeshua son of Annanias, came to Jerusalem for the feast of the Tabernacles." In the Temple he spoke in a loud voice against Jerusalem and the Temple. He was arrested by some of the leading citizens and beaten. He offered no resistance but continued to call out his warnings against the city.

The Jewish authorities took him before the Roman procurator. He was scourged by the latter unmercifully, saying nothing all the while except "Woe to Jerusalem." The procurator, Albinus, decided that he was infirm of mind and set him free.

The account has a great deal in common with the story of the trial of Jesus. He too had come to the city for a festival. He too had prophesied woe on Jerusalem and had spoken of the destruction of the Temple; he too had been tried by the Jewish authorities and taken before the procurator; he too had been scourged and had offered no defence. The very name of the victim in the story, Jeshua, recalls his own.

Only the date, the name of the procurator, and the

final release of the prisoner conflict with the Jesus story. Is it possible that this tale enshrines an orally transmitted and distorted folklore memory of the trial of Jesus, transmitted by countryfolk unfamiliar with the written records and finally written down by Josephus out of its correct historical context?[1] Josephus, repeating the tale, was trying to sketch the background to the Jews' final war against the Romans. The desolate prophecy which Jesus made about Jerusalem was fulfilled by the Roman triumph in that war, and tales of his trial, inaccurate and wrongly placed as to date, may have later been told in the countryside as providing a portent of the end of both city and Temple.

# 15

# To Each His Own

The fate of many who played their part in the tragedy of the Crucifixion is known to us. Without Judas' identification of Jesus the secret arrest would have been impossible, and to that extent Judas was the prime mover of the trials. As we know, he was later overcome with remorse, sought to return the reward of thirty silver pieces, and, in despair, hanged himself. But what prompted this remorse?

We have already made two surmises: first, that he was an ardent nationalist and had seen the events of Palm Sunday as the climax to all his hopes; second, that Caiaphas had arranged from the first that Jesus would be handed over to the Roman power. In the context of Judas' suicide we may legitimately construct a further hypothesis. Judas, angered by the realisation that Jesus was not seeking the restoration of any national kingdom, might well have decided to destroy him. Old loyalties and old affection counted for nothing. He realised that the only way to do this was to help the Temple authorities arrest Jesus. To the full plot of Caiaphas he was certainly not a party. So that he was horrified when Caiaphas decided not to deal with the prisoner himself but to hand him over to those very occupying forces which Judas hated and whose overthrow he sought. It is significant that it was only after Jesus had been led before Pontius Pilate that Judas repented and took back the thirty silver coins to the chief priests. This supports the view that it was the handing over of the prisoner to the Roman authority which caused the final disillusionment and remorse. Judas had betrayed not only his friend but the very cause which he had placed above friendship. The Jewish authorities scornfully rejected both his repentance and the silver coins. In the darkness of the final and terrible knowledge that he had caused the blood of his friend to be spilled in vain and by the agents of the imperial power which he was seeking so ardently to destroy, Judas hanged himself (Matthew 27:2–5).

Caiaphas was moved to arrest and prosecute Jesus not merely by a desire to rid the nation of a blasphemer. He was anxious to retain the support of the Roman authorities and publicly to show himself a friend of Caesar. He knew, from his experiences under the governorship of Gratus, that he could be dismissed at the mere whim of the prefect. The very vestments that he wore were released from the Antonia barracks at the prefect's pleasure. Caiaphas could strut on the world's stage only because of the Roman soldiers who stood guard in the wings and by favour of the civil authority which kept peace in the city where he played his colourful and—to an ambitious man—pleasing part. This was why he took Jesus to be tried by Pilate shortly after dawn on that first Good Friday.

The excuse that only Pilate could inflict the death penalty was weak. The Jewish religious authorities could inflict the death penalty, as we have already seen. The stoning of Stephen is evidence that the same right continued after the death of Jesus.

As far as the Sanhedrin were concerned, Jesus' offence had been that of blasphemy. But his guilt and his apparent arrogation not only of divine but kingly authority presented Caiaphas with a golden opportunity to show himself a loyal supporter of the existing regime, by bringing the criminal to the direct notice of Rome's representative. If this meant the cruel suffering and death of one man, so be it. He must have seen scores of men die by crucifixion. Experience would have dulled both his sensitivity to the horrors involved and his compassion. All that he did from dawn till noontime on Good Friday was for him merely an astute and sensible course of action. He would have given public proof of his loyalty and would enjoy more securely the wealth and influence of his high office. It is difficult to imagine that he ever looked back on that day's work with regret, still less with repentance. Sadly for Caiaphas, his zeal in Rome's cause failed him at the latter end, and the sacrifice of Jesus was, from Caiaphas' point of view, made in vain.

Within the Roman Empire it was not unusual for the

people of a province to appeal over the head of their local governor for redress of their grievances. The Jews, as we have seen, had already followed this practice and had sent a delegation to Augustus on the death of King Herod. They had done it again in the case of the tyrannical Archelaus. Some years after the Crucifixion they sent yet another delegation to negotiate for relief from the oppressions of the local regime. This time their spokesmen did not travel westwards to Rome but northwards into Syria to see the governor. The governorship at this time was held by a man named Vitellius, who was later to become emperor. To him in his palace at Antioch the Jewish spokesmen went and recounted all that they suffered. Vitellius was a just man, stern to subordinates who abused their power and compassionate towards the common people whom they oppressed. He left the comfort of his palace and undertook the journey southwards to Jerusalem to see for himself how the people of Judea were faring.

Rome had never interfered with the religious practices of the people she conquered except where religious beliefs produced barbarous atrocities. Because the Druids burned men alive as sacrifices to their strange gods, Roman armies had sought to root out the religion by force of arms in Britain and elsewhere. But normally they respected and indeed protected all provincial creeds. The Jews had caused no offence, and Vitellius was sympathetically disposed towards them. He realised that it was one thing to make kings an instrument of subjection but quite another to use religious officials for the same purpose. The action of Gratus in placing the high priest's vestments in the

Antonia, an act symbolic of the subordination of the high priest to Rome's military power, was distasteful to him. He withdrew the holy robes from the custody of the soldiers and magnanimously returned them to the Temple. Never again would there be a puppet high priest. Next, he dismissed Caiaphas ignominiously from his office, appointing Annas in his stead.[1]

So all the sycophancy which Caiaphas had displayed towards the Roman power had been in vain. The fawning part he played in bringing about the death of Jesus proved no defence against the contempt of his masters, and he ended his days in obscurity, bereft of power, glory, and high office.

Pontius Pilate, like Caiaphas, had contributed to the death of Jesus for reasons that were quite ignoble. He could not have reached the position of prefect without having received the rigid training given to all Roman officials. Many would have been the cases he had tried in the lower courts as a junior magistrate when he was young, and he would have learned much from his seniors and monitors about Roman justice and the rigidity of the law. He was too much of a Roman and too well trained to bring in a verdict of guilty against Jesus on the basis of the flimsy evidence offered. More than once he declared Jesus not guilty. This was perhaps due not only to the lack of a good case but to the complete incomprehensibility of the charge as far as Pilate was concerned. The Sanhedrin arraigned Jesus on a charge of blasphemy, but there was no such crime in Roman law. And if the Jews were charging Jesus with the offence of claiming to be the Messiah, the king of Israel, the matter seemed to be based on ancient legend and did not imply any political crime of armed rebellion. Pilate, as a trained Roman official, could not but pronounce Jesus guiltless of any crime. But he was not strong enough to risk his career by standing out against the subtle pressure of Caiaphas and his colleagues or the more unruly mob's brutal and vociferous demands.

The pressure brought by Caiaphas lay in his suggestion that Pilate's verdict of not guilty might be seen as disloyalty to the distant but all-powerful emperor. Pilate had some cause for fear. Caiaphas could take no action against Pilate in the question of blasphemy, but he could report to the governor of Syria that Pilate had been disloyal to the regime in two regards: first, that he had set free a man who had claimed to be, like the emperor, *filius divi;* second, that Pilate had freed a man who claimed to be king of the Jews—a claim in defiance of the arrangements made by the Roman authorities for the government of the province.

To the more brutal pressures of the mob, with their insistent clamour that Jesus should be crucified, Pilate could offer no resolute defiance. Just as he had ordered the retreat of the standards because of public clamour and just as he had ordered the withdrawal of the golden shields for the same reason, so now he was prepared to surrender to the mob rather than risk an outbreak of violence, with all that this might have meant to his career. He knew the abhorrence in which crucifixion was held by the Jewish people. And yet the mob was calling not merely for Jesus' death but specifically for his crucifixion. Could this be spontaneous? Did it not rather smack of a prearranged demonstration? Perhaps in the tumultuous shouting he recognised the existence of a conspiracy against him, with Caiaphas and the Sanhedrin using the city mob against him.

Pilate did not reach his final decision easily. It was not the Jews who remembered, but he who reminded them, that on the feast of the Passover it was customary to give an amnesty to a prisoner. By using one of their own customs, he hoped that he could release an innocent prisoner without raising a religious riot. But as we have seen, he was unsuccessful. The crowd continued their mindless shouts of "Crucify him!"

Pilate could see his whole career in jeopardy. If he did what justice demanded and released an innocent man, he would face considerable danger. He would win the enmity of Caiaphas, a formidable opponent, who had already hinted that he would report Pilate as no friend of Caesar's. More immediately he would have a riot on his hands, which would have been bad enough in any circumstances. But at the feast of the Passover, when the city was crammed with pilgrims, a most ugly situation could develop. If this were to happen and if he had to call out the troops, he would have to make his report to Rome, and Caiaphas apart, he would be seen as an ineffective and clumsy administrator. Therefore, as he had followed a policy of appeasement before, so he followed it now. He already had three executions on his hands for that day—two thieves and Barabbas. What did the death of one more man weigh in the balance against his whole future career? As Caiaphas had sacrificed Jesus to safeguard his position as high priest, so did Pilate sacrifice him to ensure his own professional future. But as with Caiaphas, so with Pilate, for when

Vitellius came from Syria to investigate the situation in Judea, he was satisfied that Pilate was both incompetent and tyrannous. In March, A.D. 37 (shortly after the death of Tiberius), he dismissed Pilate out of hand and sent him back to Rome to stand trial.[2]

A later author, Eusebius, tells us that rather than face trial, Pilate committed suicide. Eusebius was writing about A.D. 300 and is too late to be taken as a totally reliable witness. But his story is plausible. Suicide among the Romans was a frequent means of escaping disgrace. It was no crime but a stern man's answer to disaster and accorded well with those virtues which Rome applauded.

So, from the pages of Josephus, we may be sure that Pilate's career ended in disgrace and, from the words of Eusebius, if he were recording a more ancient tradition, that Pilate died by his own hand. So he, like Caiaphas, had sacrificed Jesus in vain.

For Herod the Tetrarch, who had set the pattern for the mockery of Jesus by dressing him in the imperial purple and who had sent him back to Pilate, a greater ignominy was reserved. Tiberius Caesar died four or five years after the Crucifixion, in A.D. 37. He was succeeded by his adopted son, Gaius Caesar, a great-grandson of Augustus. Remembered by his nickname, Caligula, he was one of the maddest of Rome's emperors. It was he who pronounced the final sentence on Herod.

Herod always resented the fact that Rome had never granted him the title of king. During the second year of Caligula's reign Herod's wife, Herodias (the same who had conspired for the death of John the Baptist), was incensed by the fact that her brother, Agrippa, a grandson of Herod the Great, had been appointed as governor of several provinces by Caligula. Agrippa had hitherto led an obscure and unsuccessful life and been forced to flee from his creditors. She considered it a gross insult to her husband that Agrippa should have been advanced so splendidly by the new emperor.

She persuaded Herod to visit Rome to seek the title of king at the emperor's hands. Agrippa learned of Herod's intentions and sent one of his freedmen, Fortunatus, to Rome with a letter to Caligula. In this letter Agrippa charged Herod with past seditions and with planning armed uprising, alleging that he had collected sufficient arms for a host of seventy thousand men.

Fortunatus presented the letter to Caligula at Baiae, a seaside resort close to Rome, before Herod had obtained an audience. When Herod was finally taken into the emperor's presence, the latter opened the conversation with a blunt question as to whether it was true that he had such a great store of arms. Taken aback, Herod admitted it. Caligula, without more ado, deprived him of his dominions and his personal fortune, both of which he gave to Agrippa as a reward. He sentenced Herod to perpetual exile in Lyons. To Herodias he showed mercy, but this mercy too was in the form of an insult, for he allowed her to retain her personal fortune for her brother Agrippa's sake, thus emphasising that Agrippa was his friend and Herod his despised enemy. So Herod and Herodias lived out their lives in perpetual exile, first in Lyons and later in Spain.[3]

Herod, who remembered the glory of his father's reign and who had himself ruled over wide lands, ended his days in poverty, far from Galilee, forced to live on his wife's bounty. Did he ever remember the man whom he had mocked when he himself was in the full glory of his power? Did the irony come home to him that he, who had all the powers of a king, had mocked his prisoner with a parody of the regalia of kingship and sent him to his death and that now he, the onetime tetrarch, had lost his dominions? Gone now was the sceptre he bore and gone were the fine garments he had worn, a travesty of which he had caused to be thrown over the shoulders of the man who, a brief few years ago, had lain at his mercy.

So the chief players in the drama, those who were most instrumental in putting Jesus to death, were themselves in turn broken on the wheel of fortune. But there was another collective presence at the trial which influenced events and which made inevitable the sentence of death by crucifixion. This was the city of Jerusalem, personified by the crowds which thronged its streets, which attended the public examination of Jesus, and which, when Pilate sought to set him free, made the streets of the city ring with their savage clamour of "Crucify him, crucify him!"

During those last few days in Jerusalem, between Palm Sunday and that second Passover where Jesus himself was the paschal lamb, he had realised with unaccustomed bitterness the part which the city was playing in the drama. In the Temple he had openly rebuked the scribes and Pharisees. He referred to Jerusalem as a city which had killed the prophets and stoned them (Matthew 23:37). He was moved to weep over the city and to foretell the day when it would be besieged by enemies. Trenches of war would be dug about the city, which would finally be laid level with the earth. The Temple itself would be destroyed, and not one stone would be left standing on another. Just as retribution came to the human figures in the drama, so did it come to the city itself, in a manner that almost precisely fulfilled the words of Jesus.

Some thirty years after the Crucifixion, Nero Caesar died. By his day the Christians in Rome formed a large enough communtiy to cause anxiety to the authorities, and it was during his reign that the first major persecution of those Christians began.

He was the last of the line of Julius Caesar to reign over the imperial city. On his death there was civil war, with three rival military commanders contending for power. Vespasian was at that time governor of Syria. The Jews had rejected the Messianic claims of Jesus and still believed that a great ruler was to be born to them. These beliefs found their way into the Roman world in a garbled fashion. They came to the ears of Vespasian in Antioch in the form that a great ruler should arise from the East. Encouraged by these portents, he marched his legions to Rome, seized power, and declared himself Caesar. Because of his close links with Judea, which had come under his jurisdiction as governor of Syria, he resolved to deal harshly with the Jews.

He sent his son Titus (who was to become emperor in his turn) to Judea with a large army. Titus besieged Jerusalem, encompassing it with a trench, and brought his great engines of war and the might of the legions against the city walls. Despite the most gallant defence put up by the Jews, the city fell, and the Temple, save only for one wall, was destroyed. Not one stone was left standing on another. Vespasian jubilantly struck a special silver coin to commemorate his son's feat. The coin showed a Roman soldier standing triumphantly over a mourning figure representing Judea, sitting sorrowfully under a palm tree. It is inscribed with the word "Judea."

By that defeat, the Jews lost not only their kingdom but their homeland. From that day they were scattered over the face of the earth, and it was to be nearly two thousand years before they were to return as a nation. The one wall of the Temple remains to this day, the Wailing Wall, an enduring memorial to the fate which overcame the city at the hands of the legions of Titus. And it commemorates the bitter words of Jesus.

# 16

# The Final Triumph

Rome, through its delegate Pontius Pilate, had inflicted on Jesus the most savage and humiliating death in all its repertory of punishments. For Jews and Romans alike, the cross was a symbol of shame. No free Roman might be executed on it. It was a doom reserved for baser men and slaves. For the Jews, the body of any man who had died in this way was defiled and accursed. And yet less than three hundred years after the Crucifixion the cross was to become the imperial badge and, on shield and standard, was to replace the proud eagles which had presided over Rome's destiny for a thousand years.

The apostles remained steadfast in their loyalty to Jesus as their leader and teacher and to their unshakeable belief that he had risen from the tomb and had ascended into heaven. They saw him now not merely as the Son of God but as God himself. The doctrine of the Trinity was swift in growing. God himself consisted of God the Father, of God the Son, and of the Holy Spirit. Jesus, in his aspect of God the Son, was therefore identifiable with the Creator himself.

To Orthodox Jews, with their strict belief in the uniqueness of God, such a doctrine was totally repugnant. Had the apostles limited their labours to converting their fellow Jews to their own beliefs, Christianity would never have flourished as one of the great religions of the world. It might have ended as it began, as a subsect of the Jewish faith.

This indeed was how it was seen by contemporary observers immediately after the Crucifixion, for the apostles, following the example of their leader, continued to visit the Temple and to teach his doctrines there. But they went further. They proclaimed Jesus to be a descendant of David whom the latter had promised he would raise up as the Anointed One to sit on his throne (Acts 2:30). But Peter also told the Jews that in Jesus they had crucified someone who was both the Lord and their king, the Anointed One, the Christ (Acts 2:36).

The number of their followers grew, and very swiftly they were numbered in their thousands. Their work, like that of Jesus himself, attracted the suspicious opposition of the Temple authorities. More than once they were imprisoned but were released miraculously, according to the Gospels. The Temple authorities forbore from bringing them to open trial—perhaps because they did not wish to repeat what in retrospect must have appeared their cruel treatment of Jesus, or perhaps the very success of the movement and the dramatic new authority with which the disciples appeared to be invested caused at least some of them to think that it may have come from God. So despite this opposition, the number of their followers grew. They were recognised as men of a distinct faith and became known as the Nazarenes. The apostles were swiftly successful in rebuilding the apparently shattered work of Jesus and in persuading many of their fellow Jews that their Anointed One had lived unrecognised among them. Through the gateway of death, he had now entered into the invisible kingdom over which he and his Father presided. But, given the political stresses which we have examined and the self-interest of the official council and priesthood, it was not possible to bring these beliefs universally to all the inhabitants of Jerusalem, let alone to all Judeans. So although the sect of the Nazarenes increased (to a number of some 5,000), the vast majority of the Jews rejected and still reject the idea that Jesus was the Anointed One and their king in either a temporal or spiritual sense.

Despite these obstacles and despite the total unacceptability to Orthodox Jews of the idea of the Trinity, such was the drive and single-mindedness of the apostles that the faith stubbornly survived in Jerusalem itself. In the days of Jesus there was little or no formal organisation of the apostles or of their followers. (The most we are told of any formal appointments among the apostles is that Judas looked after their funds.) They were a group of dedicated friends, believing in and disseminating the teachings of their master without any formal hierarchy or division of responsibilities.

But after the Crucifixion the apostles began to introduce a certain amount of formality. Peter, for example, became the *episcopus*—or overseer—of the followers of Jesus in Jerusalem. Because they completely accepted the promise given to them by Jesus that he would be present wherever two or three were gathered together in his name, the assembling of his followers became a matter of prime importance. The Greek word for assembly is *ecclesia.* The word "church" is an old English word for an assembly, which was used when the Scriptures were first translated into English long before the Norman Conquest. These assemblies were the formal body within which the teachings of Jesus were to be maintained until he came again. For the existence of a formal church of Jerusalem (an organised assembly in a special building) evidence is scant.

Despite the success of the Nazarenes in sustaining the impetus of the teachings of Jesus, they could not hope to capture the citadel of orthodoxy of the Temple or to convert all their coreligionists to their new and still strange beliefs. It seemed that there were two alternatives for the infant church: It might have remained as a prosperous but minor sect of Jewry, exercising some influence on the mainstream of Jewish thought, or after a generation or two it might have lost its original momentum and merged into the general body of Jewish belief, carrying at best a few traces of its founder's teaching.

In fact history offered the church a third possibility. It could seek to escape from the limitations of Jewish orthodoxy and teach the new faith to pagan nations who, unlike the Jews, had no deeply held faith of their own and who were seeking answers to questions about the relationship of man with the divine powers. This was made possible by the very power which had put Jesus to death. All roads led to Rome, and all the sea lanes of the world led to the imperial city. We have seen how swiftly delegations of Jews could attend upon the emperor on the Palatine Hill to discuss their grievances. Imperial communications were excellent, and in time Peter was able himself to go to Rome, to become bishop, and ultimately to die there for his faith. Paul, the apostle who had never seen Jesus, also visited Rome and was imprisoned there. It was he who had argued that the message of the new Messiah had to be carried not only to the Jewish people but to the pagans who inhabited the Roman world.

At first the church in Rome seemed to the authorities to be no more than a sect of the large Jewish population which the Romans had long been accustomed to see in their midst. This is not surprising, since initially all the Christians were of the Jewish faith. Converts had to undergo the rite of circumcision, and like Orthodox Jews, they observed the Sabbath and followed the law. Tacitus tells us how Emperor Claudius in A.D. 49 expelled the Jews from Rome as a result of disturbances which took place *impulsante Chresto*—"at the instigation of a man named Chrestos."[1] His words show a noticeable Christian community in Rome within fifteen or sixteen years of the Crucifixion. They show that the Roman authorities saw them as a Jewish sect. They indicate that the administration of Claudius thought of

Christ (about whose name they were uncertain) as a man still alive, leading his followers to violence and unrest.

We know also that the new faith spread in Rome among people of all classes and made its way even into Caesar's own palace. For Paul, writing to the Romans, sends his greetings to those of the faithful "in the household of Caesar" (Philippians 4:22).

While Peter and his followers were busy building the infant assembly of Christians (the *ecclesia,* or church, in Rome), the indefatigable Paul was using the communications network of the empire to preach his news of the living God in Greece and Asia Minor. A century and a half later Origen was to write that God had subjected all the nations of the world to the Caesars in order that they might be made ready to receive the message of Christ. Certainly, although it was Rome who put Jesus to death, it was through the instrument of her empire that Christianity was able to spread so widely and rapidly.

The new faith had much to offer first-century Rome and her subjects. The old gods had become unreal figures in fairy tales and dreams. Men had grown world-weary, dissatisfied with the pleasures of the flesh and finding no answers to those questions which have troubled man since first he walked upright, as to his origins, his relationship with the universe, and the fate that would befall him when life departed and nothing seemed left except a pale and putrefying corpse. The Greeks had sought answers in intellectual philosophies which, however noble, left the common man unsatisfied and made little impression on the customs and standards of society as a whole. Human life, whatever the Stoics might preach, was still held in contempt. Society accepted that some men were free and some men were slaves, the mere tools and victims of their masters. The promise of Christianity came as a revelation. Rapidly it ceased to be a mere sect of the Jews. It became recognisable as a new religion.

It swiftly spread far beyond the shores of the Mediterranean. In Britain, the most distant and isolated province of the empire, there were legends that the new faith came very early. Mark tells us (15:42–6) that one Joseph, a native of Ramathaim (Joseph of Arimathea), was an honourable councillor, suggesting that he was a member of the Sanhedrin. According to Matthew (27:57–60), he was a follower of Jesus and arranged for burial to be given to the latter's pitiful and broken body after it was removed from the cross. Legend tells us that later he went to Britain, bringing with him the crown of thorns, the spear with which the side of Jesus had been pierced, and either the cup or the dish used at the last Passover feast. The details of the legend are improbable, and the dates when it was recorded are late. But the story is not impossible to believe. By causing the body of a criminal to be honourably buried, he would have earned the odium of his colleagues in the Sanhedrin and of the Roman authorities. Since it was far from his own tomb that the Resurrection was said to have taken place and since the Resurrection became the central theme of the new faith, both the Jewish and Roman authorities would have seen him as having played a key and unwelcome part in the foundation of a new and troublesome sect. If he found it necessary to leave

Judea, to what better place could he flee than Britain? Cut off by sea from the central authority, it would have provided a safe refuge as well as a civilised and Romanised environment. So he is said to have come to the island province and to have built a church in Glastonbury dedicated to the mother of Jesus. Thither he brought the cup (which became the Holy Grail of legend) and the crown of thorns, from which he planted a cutting. To this day a thorn tree grows at Glastonbury which is said to blossom at Christmastime and which by many is held to be a descendant of that first cutting.

The reputed dedication of the church seems to argue against the validity of the legend. If Joseph had left Judea immediately after the Crucifixion, Mary was probably still alive. Moreover, churches built during the first fifty years of Christianity were probably not dedicated to saints but only to God.

But to stand in the ruins of the little church and to feel the special atmosphere which has always surrounded Glastonbury is to be so charmed by the legend as to believe, in spite of the absence of direct and reliable evidence, that some historical events, now obscured by the mists and darkness of myth, have given this spot some special place in the annals of Christianity.

The second link between Britain and the early church is more positive. When Roman legions finally conquered the island, during the reign of Claudius in A.D. 43, they were commanded by Aulus Plautius, whose career is well documented by Tacitus and by Dio. After the fighting was over, he remained in Britain as governor. On his return to Rome, he was given an ovation, the equivalent of a triumph, and received an expression of personal gratitude from Claudius Caesar himself.

Some years later, during the reign of Nero, his wife, Pomponia Graecina, was accused of having followed what Tacitus calls "a foreign superstition."[2] It is interesting and may be significant that Tacitus uses the same word *superstitio* to describe Christianity in the account which he gives in another place of Nero's persecution of the Christians.[3] Suetonius, a later writer, also uses the word *superstitio* about the new faith.[4] Normally Rome was very tolerant of foreign religions. The troops brought back many gods from the provinces. Isis, Cybele, and Mithras were but a few of the alien divinities worshipped by the Romans. Their devotees stood in no risk of legal action, nor were their various faiths seen as superstitions.

Further, the charge against Pomponia Graecina was brought during Nero's reign, and we know that he persecuted the Christians. This, coupled with Tacitus' phrase, has long been interpreted as indicating that she was charged with being a Christian. Aulus Plautius was allowed to try the case himself and found her not guilty.

There is one further piece of evidence. Tacitus tells us that she lived to a great age and that the last forty years of her life were spent in perpetual mourning for the loss of her friend Julia, who had been put to death as the result of a plot by Messalina.[5] But to mourn forty years for a friend is, at the very least, odd. Might she not rather have been leading the withdrawn life of a religious? Finally, her family name is to be found in the catacombs, so that kinsmen of hers were among the early Christians in Rome.

There is another matter which could link her with the new faith about which speculation began in the eighteenth century. While Aulus Plautius was in Britain, he appointed Cogidumnus, a local king, as representative of the imperial power. Cogidumnus is mentioned by Tacitus as an example of the manner in which Rome used local kings as instruments of power. There is also a stone in Chichester Museum bearing his name, which shows that Cogidumnus had adopted the additional name of Claudius, presumably in honour of the emperor. The stone commemorates the dedication of a temple to Minerva, the land for which was given by one Clementinus, son of Pudentinus.

During the first century the poet Martial wrote an epithalamium celebrating the marriage of a girl named Claudia to a man name Pudens, describing Claudia as a *peregrina,* that is to say, the citizen of a Roman province.[6] In a later poem there is another reference to a woman named Claudia, a wife and mother.[7] She is generally accepted as being the same Claudia as the bride referred to in the earlier verses. Her husband (and if she is indeed the same person, then this would be Pudens) is described as *sanctus,* a holy husband. But this word *sanctus,* or holy, was used to describe all members of the early church. Many of the apostolic Epistles are addressed "to the saints." Finally, Martial's second poem specifically tells us that Claudia hailed from Britain. Were Claudia and Pudens Christians? The classical name Claudia would be unusual in Britain at this early date, but any daughter of Claudius Cogidumnus might well have been so named. Clearly the soldier Clementinus Pudentinus knew King Cogidumnus. The name of Claudia's husband, Pudens, suggests that he might have been the son or kinsman of Clementinus, who was the son of a man named Pudentinus. This would explain not only the names of the bride and bridegroom but how it was that a Roman had come to marry a Briton.

If Pomponia Graecina had visited Britain during her husband's governorship, she might well have honoured Rome's client king by visiting him and by getting to know his daughter. If so, Claudia might well have been converted to Christianity by no less a personage than the governor's wife.

Point is given to the speculation by Paul's Second Epistle to Timothy. Among those listed as sending their greetings are a Pudens and a Claudia, who are thus clearly identified as Christians. To find the same two names coupled in Martial's poem and again in Paul's Epistle strongly suggests that the same two people are involved. To find the names Claudius Cogidumnus and Clementinus, son of Pudentinus, mentioned together on a stone from Britain, when we know that Claudia was a Briton, is equally suggestive. So perhaps Pomponia Graecina brought the news of Jesus to the far land of Britain, and perhaps the crucified king was worshipped in the island province within twenty years of the Crucifixion.

Legend and speculation apart, we know from reliable sources with what bewildering speed the new faith had spread through the Roman world. The destroyed city of Pompeii provides some evidence. Pompeii was overwhelmed by an eruption of Vesuvius in A.D. 79. Therefore everything found there must have existed before that date, that is to say, within thirty-five years or so of the Crucifixion. In 1925, in one of the houses of Pompeii, there was discovered an acrostic word square, which is in fact a coded reference to the *Pater Noster* (Our Father) and to the Greek letters alpha and omega, which were early taken by Christians as a symbol of the Godhead.[8]

At Herculaneum (a sister town of Pompeii, overwhelmed in the same disaster) there has been found in the upper room of a house a wooden cupboard with a tablelike top which has been taken to be an altar. On the floor before it is a small pavement of brickwork on which the worshipper might stand and kneel. On the wall above it is a cruciform space where once a cross had been set, possibly in metal, but now long since vanished. This has often been supposed to be a Christian altar.[9]

By the middle of the second century Emperor Hadrian refers in his letters with some admiration to the followers of Jesus. He points to the democratic manner whereby bishops were elected and draws a political moral therefrom.

Under his successor, Trajan, the Christians continued to be persecuted for their obduracy in refusing to worship any God but their own and for refusing to pay their religious respects to the divine spirits of Rome and the emperor. Trajan's governor in Bithynia was the author Pliny the Younger, who, as a humane and reasonable man, found his task of executing Christians very distasteful. So he put two Christian slave girls to the torture—for the most scientific and humane reasons! He wanted to wring from them the truth about this strange and secret cult, to find out whether they truly deserved punishment. They gave him, according to his letter to Trajan (which survives), an outline of a Christian meeting or service. All would join in prayer, would renew their oaths not to steal, not to rob, not to commit adultery, not to break their faith—all of which sounds like a reference to the recital of the Ten Commandments. All would later eat together in friendship. Trajan's reply also survives. He instructed Pliny not to go out of his way to seek out Christians but to punish only those who were obdurate. Nor was he to take notice of anonymous accusations. The slave girls had not suffered in vain.

Despite this growth of the faith, there is archaeological evidence for a mocking attitude to Christians at this time. There has been discovered on a wall in the palace of Trajan a roughly sketched caricature of a crucified man. The figure on the cross bears an ass' head. Beneath the cartoon are inscribed the words "Alexamenas worships his god."[10] It would seem that there was still confusion between Christians and Jews in the minds of the Romans, for whoever made the drawing evidently had in mind the reference to the idea expressed by Tacitus that the ass was sacred to the Jews. We must also remember that the ass was, then as now, the symbol of the stupid, the obstinate, and the contemptible!

By their fortitude under persecution, by their unshakeable loyalty to their beliefs, and by the compassionate hope of their message, the Christian community prospered and its message was heard by the great ones of Rome. Marcia, concubine of Emperor Commodus (who died in A.D. 192), was an avowed

Christian. Alexander Severus, who was emperor from A.D. 222 to 235, is said to have placed a figure of Jesus among his household gods.

The new faith, however humble its beginnings, had much to offer Rome and her empire. For centuries the Roman people had been seeking to discover the relationship between man and the immortals. Abstruse Greek philosophy was not for them. They held the Greeks in awe, admired their intellectual skills, but nevertheless derided them as intellectual babblers. Their own gods had become mere folklore figures rather than true divinities. Perhaps in the country places (as the poet Tibullus teaches us) reality still lurked behind the worship of rustic gods. But for the urban population throughout the empire the old gods had virtually ceased to be. Men were eagerly seeking some faith to explain the cruelties of the world and to give promise of peace and salvation. Devotees of the god Mithras accepted baptism in the blood of a bull to win the favours of their god and to gain salvation. Others, in religious frenzy, castrated themselves to placate the goddess Cybele. Others again worshipped Isis and the gods of Egypt. There were those who followed the cult of Adonis, who was killed each year and who rose again from death to immortal life.

To this frustrated and anxious society the offer of Christianity made an irresistible appeal. For the slaves there was the message of a compassionate God who saw all mankind as his children. For the rich there was divine reassurance against the sense of earthly insecurity which bedevilled all. For the worshippers of Mithras there was a faith that had much in common with their own but from which the harsh baptism of blood and the warlike metaphor of God's legions were absent. For the worshippers of Adonis there was a resurrection from the tomb which had been witnessed and recorded. For all there was the knowledge that the new God, like the gods of old, was always present, had walked the earth in human form, and was still a living force despite having suffered an earthly death.

By the early fourth century two religions dominated the empire. The army worshipped Mithras, the Lord of Light, whose origins lay in Persia and whose cult, some said, had been brought to Rome by prisoners taken by Pompey half a century before the birth of Jesus. Wherever the army marched, they took Mithras with them. Statues of the young god, wearing his Phrygian cap, are to be found wherever a garrison was stationed. From Hadrian's Wall, from the city of London, from France and from Spain such figures come. The vanished legions left numerous portrayals of their warlike and tutelary divinity.

For the most part the civilian population followed the Nazarene. Within the civil service Christianity made particular progress. During her wars against Greece, Rome had taken and enslaved many Greek prisoners. These were better educated than their masters, more skilled in administration and the arts of communication. So the civil service came to be manned largely by slaves or freedmen of this kind. As slaves, they welcomed the promise of the new faith. As Greeks, they could understand and appreciate the subtleties of the Trinity, the oracular sayings of the prophets, and the mysteries which had begun to surround the Christian faith.

There was by now a division in the imperial government. The old days of a single world ruler had vanished. The empire had two capitals, one in Constantinople and one in Rome. In each sat an Augustus Caesar, each with his junior, selected by him as assistant and successor, who bore the name of Caesar. Diocletian, the most dominant of the four rulers of Rome and who reigned from A.D. 284 to 305, saw Christianity as a growing threat to the state. A military man, his coinage bears slogans extolling Mithras, the army's chosen god. He declared war on Christianity in the last and perhaps the most vicious of all the persecutions. Churches were dismantled, copies of the Bible destroyed, priests hunted down and executed. It was during this time that Saint Alban, the first recorded British martyr, was killed.

Diocletian was followed by Constantine, the son of his colleague, Constantius Chlorus. Constantine had begun his career in Britain. There he dreamed of restoring the days when one man ruled supreme. He led the legions out of Britain, and after a long and complicated campaign he brought them to the gates of Rome. As he lay in camp, he knew that the morrow's battle would decide his fate—triumph or disaster. Later he said that he had seen a vision in the sky (by some accounts a cross, by others Christ's monogram) with the words *In hoc signo vinces*—"In this sign thou shalt conquer!" That night he caused his soldiers to replace their eagle standards with new ones bearing Christ's monogram. The military insignia on their shields were painted over and replaced with Christian symbols. The next day he conquered his opponents and entered Rome.

He was most anxious to record his vision for posterity and made a solemn declaration about it to a Christian bishop, Eusebius. However, cynics have suggested that in changing his army's standards from pagan to Christian symbols, Constantine was politically rather than spiritually motivated. He had already gained the army's loyalty. It was vital, should he enter Rome as a victor, that he should win the support of the city's population and of the civil servants. How better to do this than to declare his support of the Christian God! There is some evidence to support this interpretation. He did not accept baptism until he was advanced in years and was facing approaching death. Moreover, his coins, even those dated long after his victory, continued to bear Mithraic slogans and to describe him as the Companion of the Unconquered Sun.

Shortly after his victorious entry into Rome he declared Christianity to be a lawful religion and endowed the church with lands and riches. Increasingly the Cross, once the symbol of shame, became the badge of Rome's sovereignty. As during classical times she had been the heart and centre of the civilised world, achieving that position by force of arms, so in mediaeval days, after Constantine's actions, she became the heart and centre of Christianity by the tradition of her first bishop, Peter, and by her historical inheritance.

So the story that had begun so humbly in the stable at Bethlehem and that had reached its climax in the darkness and horror of the Crucifixion ended triumphantly in the imperial city.

# Notes

*Preface*

1. Josef Blinzler, *The Trial of Jesus* (London: Newman Press, 1959), p. 30.

*1. A Crowd of Gods*

1. Julius Caesar, *de Bello Gallico* (London: William Heinemann Ltd., 1917), VI, 16–28.
2. *Ibid.*, VI, 21.
3. Tacitus, *Germania* (London: William Heinemann Ltd., 1969), IX.
4. *Ibid.*, XLIII.
5. Tacitus, *Annales* (London: William Heinemann Ltd., 1931), II, 60.
6. Tacitus, *Historiae* (London: William Heinemann Ltd., 1925), V, 9.

2. *Judea—the Roman Province*

1. Juvenal, *Satirae* (London: William Heinemann Ltd., 1918), VI, v. 158.
2. Pliny, *Historiae Naturalis* (London: William Heinemann Ltd., 1945), XIII, 4.
3. Horace, *Satirae* (London: William Heinemann Ltd., 1929), I, 5.
4. *Ibid.*, I, 9.
5. Persius, *Satirae* (London: William Heinemann Ltd., 1918), V, 114.
6. Tacitus, *Historiae*, V.
7. *Ibid.*, V, 4.
8. Tacitus, *Agricola* (London: William Heinemann Ltd., 1969), XIV.
9. Josephus, *De Antiquitatis Judaeorum* (London: J. Walker, 1786), XV, 5.

3. *The Old Kingdom and the New*

1. E. and H. Leigh, *Analecta Caesarum Romanorum.*

5. *Pontius Pilate*

1. Josephus, *De Bello Judaico* (London: J. Walker, 1786), II, 118, 433.
2. Josephus, *De Antiquitatis Judaeorum*, XVII, 15.
3. F. F. Bruce, *New Testament History* (London: Oliphants Ltd., 1971),p. 16.
4. Philo, *Legatio* (London: William Heinemann Ltd., 1962), 301.
5. Josephus, *De Antiquitatis Judaeorum*, XVII.

6. *The Baptism by Water*

1. Ovid, *Fasti* (London: William Heinemann Ltd., 1931), II, 45.
2. Josephus, *De Antiquitatis Judaeorum*, XVII, 2.
3. *Ibid.*, XVIII, 7.

12. *Palm Sunday*

1. Josephus, *De Antiquitatis Judaeorum*, XVII, 9.

14. *The Three Trials*

1. Josephus, *De Bello Judaico*, VI, 302.

15. *To Each His Own*

1. Josephus, *De Antiquitatis Judaeorum*, XVIII.
2. *Ibid.*, XVIII, 35, 95.
3. *Ibid.*, XVIII, 9.

16. *The Final Triumph*

1. Tacitus, *Annales*, XIII, 32.
2. *Ibid.*, XIII, 32.
3. *Ibid.*, XV, 44.
4. Suetonius, *Nero Claudius Caesar* (London: William Heinemann Ltd., 1914), XVI.
5. Tactitus, *Annales*, XIII, 32.
6. Martial, *Poems* (London: William Heinemann Ltd., 1919), IV, 13.
7. *Ibid.*, XI, 53.

8. *Archiv für Religionswissenschaft,* XXIX, 1926.

9. Marcel Brion, *Pompeii and Herculaneum: The Glory and the Grief* (London: Elek Books Ltd., 1960), p. 86.

10. P. Carrington, *The Early Christian Church* (Cambridge, Eng.: The University Press, 1957), II, p. 396.

# Bibliography

*Archiv für Religionswissenschaft,* Vol. XXIX, 1926.

Blinzler, Joseph. *The Trial of Jesus.* London: Newman Press, 1959.

Brion, Marcel. *Pompeii and Herculaneum: The Glory and the Grief.* London: Elek Books Ltd., 1960.

Bruce, F. F. *New Testament History.* London: Oliphants Ltd., 1971.

Carrington, P. *The Early Christian Church.* Cambridge, Eng.: The University Press, 1957.

Josephus. *De Antiquitatis Judaeorum.* London: J. Walker, 1786.

Josephus. *De Bello Judaico.* London: J. Walker, 1786.

Knox, Monsignor Ronald A. Note to his translation of Luke. London: Burns and Oates Ltd., 1965.

Leigh, E. and H. *Analecta Caesarum Romanorum.* London: John Williams, 1664.

Perowne, Stewart. *Jesualem and Bethlehem.* London: J. M. Dent & Sons Ltd., 1965.

Tibullus. *Poems.* Oxford: Oxford University Press, 1914.

All the following published by Loeb Classical Library of William Heinemann Ltd. in London and by Harvard University Press in Cambridge, Massachusetts.

Caesar, Julius. *De Bello Gallico.*

Horace, *Satirae.*

Martial. *Poems.*

Ovid. *Fasti.*

Perseus. *Satirae.*

Philo, *Legatio.*

Pliny. *Historiae Naturalis.*

Suetonius. *D. Octavius Caesar Augustus.*

———. *D. Vespasianus Augustus.*

Tacitus. *Agricola.*

———. *Annales,* Books I-VI and XI-XVI.

———. *Germania.*

———. *Historiae.*